SECOND EDITION

Bash Pocket Reference

Arnold Robbins

Beijing · Boston · Farnham · Sebastopol · Tokyo

Bash Pocket Reference

by Arnold Robbins

Published by O'Reilly Media, Inc., 1005 Gravenstein Highway North, Sebastopol, CA 95472.

O'Reilly books may be purchased for educational, business, or sales promotional use. Online editions are also available for most titles (*http://safaribooksonline.com*). For more information, contact our corporate/institutional sales department: 800-998-9938 or *corporate@oreilly.com*.

Editor: Andy Oram
Production Editor: Kristen Brown
Proofreader: Jasmine Kwityn
Indexer: Arnold Robbins
Interior Designer: David Futato
Cover Designer: Karen Montgomery
Illustrator: Rebecca Demarest

March 2016:   Second Edition

Revision History for the Second Edition

2016-02-17:   First Release
2016-05-13:   Second Release

See   *http://oreilly.com/catalog/errata.csp?isbn=9781491941591*   for   release details.

978-1-491-94159-1

[LSI]

Table of Contents

The Bash Shell   1

Conventions   2
History   2
Overview of Features   3
Invoking the Shell   4
Command Exit Status   6
Syntax   7
Functions   23
Variables   25
Arithmetic Expressions   47
Command History   49
Programmable Completion   54
Job Control   59
Shell Options   60
Command Execution   66
Coprocesses   68
Restricted Shells   69
Built-In Commands   70
Resources   133
Acknowledgments   134
Acknowledgments from the First Edition   134

Index   135

The Bash Shell

This pocket reference covers Bash, particularly version 4.4, the primary shell for GNU/Linux and Mac OS X. Bash is available for Solaris and the various BSD systems, and can be easily compiled for just about any other Unix system. It can even be compiled for OpenVMS! The following topics are covered:

- History
- Overview of features
- Invoking the shell
- Command exit status
- Syntax
- Functions
- Variables
- Arithmetic expressions
- Command history
- Programmable completion
- Job control
- Shell options
- Command execution

- Coprocesses
- Restricted shells
- Built-in commands
- Resources

Conventions

Filenames, command names, options, and inline examples are shown in `constant width`. Input that a user should type in exactly as-is is shown in **`constant width userinput`**. Text that should be replaced with real data in examples and syntax descriptions is shown in *`constant width replaceable`*. New terms and emphasized words and phrases are shown in *italics*. Finally, references of the form *name*(N) refer to the manual page for *name* in section *N* of the online manual (accessed via the `man` command). Shell variable values (including environment variables) are indicated as $VAR.

History

The original Bourne shell distributed with V7 Unix in 1979 became the standard shell for writing shell scripts. The Bourne shell is still found in */bin/sh* on many commercial Unix systems. It has not changed that much since its initial release, although it has seen modest enhancements over the years. The most notable new features added were the CDPATH variable and a built-in `test` command with System III (circa 1980), command hashing and shell functions for System V Release 2 (circa 1984), and the addition of job control features for System V Release 4 (1989).

Because the Berkeley C shell (`csh`) offered features that were more pleasant for interactive use, such as command history and job control, for a long time the standard practice in the Unix world was to use the Bourne shell for programming and the C shell for daily use. David Korn at Bell Labs was the first developer to enhance the Bourne shell by adding csh-like features to it: history, job control, and additional programmability. Eventually, the Korn shell's feature set surpassed both that of the Bourne and C shells, while remaining compatible with the former for shell programming. Today, the POSIX standard defines the "standard shell" language and behavior based on the System V Bourne shell, with a selected subset of features from the Korn shell.

The Free Software Foundation, in keeping with its goal to produce a complete Unix work-alike system, developed a clone of the Bourne shell, written from scratch, named "Bash," the Bourne-Again SHell. Over time, Bash has become a POSIX-compliant version of the shell with many additional features overlapping those of the Korn shell, but Bash is not an exact Korn shell clone. Today, Bash is probably the most widely used Bourne-derived shell.

Overview of Features

The Bash shell provides the following features:

- Input/output redirection
- Wildcard characters for filename abbreviation
- Shell variables and options for customizing the environment
- A built-in command set for writing shell programs
- Shell functions, for modularizing tasks within a shell program
- Job control
- Command-line editing (using the command syntax of either vi or Emacs)
- Access to previous commands (command history) and the ability to edit them
- Integer arithmetic

- Arrays and arithmetic expressions
- Command-name abbreviation (aliasing)
- Upwards compliance with POSIX
- Internationalization facilities
- An arithmetic `for` loop

Invoking the Shell

The command interpreter for the Bash shell (`bash`) can be invoked as follows:

```
bash [options] [arguments]
```

Bash can execute commands from a terminal, from a file (when the first *argument* is a script), or from standard input (if no arguments remain or if -s is specified). The shell automatically prints prompts if standard input is a terminal, or if -i is given on the command line.

On many systems, */bin/sh* is a link to Bash. When invoked as `sh`, Bash acts more like the traditional Bourne shell: login shells read */etc/profile* and *~/.profile*, and regular shells read $ENV, if it is set. Full details are available in the *bash*(1) manpage.

Command-Line Options

Almost all the single-letter command-line options may also be used with the built-in `set` command (see the entry for `set` on page 113). The options are:

-c *str*
    Read commands from string *str*.

-D, --dump-strings
    Print all $"..." strings in the program.

- `-i`   Create an interactive shell (prompt for input). May not be used with `set`.

- `-l, --login`
  Behave as a login shell.

- `-O` *option*
  Enable `shopt` option *option*. Use `+O` to unset *option*.

- `-p`   Start up as a privileged user. Do not read `$ENV` or `$BASH_ENV`; do not import functions from the environment; and ignore the values of the `BASHOPTS`, `CDPATH`, `GLOBIGNORE`, and `SHELLOPTS` variables. The normal fixed-name startup files (such as *~/.bash_profile*) are read.

- `-r, --restricted`
  Create a restricted shell (see the section "Restricted Shells" on page 69).

- `-s`   Read commands from standard input. Output from built-in commands goes to file descriptor 1; all other shell output goes to file descriptor 2.

- `-v, --verbose`
  Print lines as the shell reads them.

- `--debugger`
  If the debugging profile is available at startup, read it and turn on the `extdebug` option to `shopt`. For use by the Bash debugger (see *http://bashdb.sourceforge.net*).

- `--dump-po-strings`
  Same as `-D`, but output in GNU `gettext` format.

- `--help`
  Print a usage message and exit successfully.

- `--init-file` *file*, `--rcfile` *file*
  Use *file* as the startup file instead of *~/.bashrc* for interactive shells.

--noediting

> Do not use the *readline* library for input, even in an inter-
> active shell.

--noprofile

> Do not read */etc/profile* or any of the personal startup files.

--norc

> Do not read *~/.bashrc*. Enabled automatically when
> invoked as sh.

--posix

> Turn on POSIX mode.

--version

> Print a version message and exit.

-, --

> End option processing.

See the entry for set on page 113 for the remaining options.

Arguments

Arguments are assigned to the positional parameters $1, $2, etc.
If the first argument is a script, commands are read from it,
and the remaining arguments are assigned to $1, $2, and so on.
The name of the script is available as $0. The script file itself
need not be executable, but it must be readable.

Command Exit Status

When any command exits, it provides a numeric *exit status* or
return value. External commands, such as ls, provide this
value to the operating system. Internal commands, such as cd,
provide this value directly to the shell.

The shell automatically retrieves the return value when the
command exits. An exit status of zero is defined, by convention, to mean *true* or *success*. Any other status means *false* or

failure. This is how the shell makes use of commands in its control flow statements such as `if`, `while`, and `until`.

Additionally, the shell makes the return value of the last executed command available in `$?` where your shell script may access it. Usually you should save it in another variable, since subsequent commands that are part of your script will overwrite it.

Exit values may range from 0 to 255. The shell uses specific numeric values to indicate certain conditions:

Numeric value	Meaning
0	Success
2	Returned by built-in commands to indicate usage errors
126	Command was found but was not executable
127	Command not found
$128 + N$	Command died due to receiving signal number N

Syntax

This section describes the many symbols peculiar to the shell. The topics are arranged as follows:

- Special files
- Filename metacharacters
- Brace expansion
- Escape sequences
- Quoting
- Command forms
- Redirection forms

Special Files

The shell reads one or more startup files. Some of the files are read only when a shell is a login shell. Bash reads these files, in this order:

- */etc/profile*. Executed automatically at login.
- The first file found from this list: *~/.bash_profile*, *~/.bash_login*, or *~/.profile*. Executed automatically at login.
- *~/.bashrc* is read by every nonlogin shell. However, if invoked as sh, or with --posix, Bash instead reads $ENV, for POSIX compatibility.

The getpwnam() and getpwuid() C library functions are the sources of home directories for *~name* abbreviations. (On personal systems, the user database is stored in */etc/passwd*. However, on networked systems, this information may come from NIS, NIS+, LDAP, or some other source, not your workstation password file.)

When an interactive login shell exits, or when non-interactive login shell executes the exit built-in command, Bash reads and executes *~/.bash_logout* if that file exists. (A login shell is one where the -l option is set.)

Filename Metacharacters

*	Match any string of zero or more characters.
?	Match any single character.
[*abc*...]	Match any one of the enclosed characters; a hyphen can specify a range (e.g., a-z, A-Z, 0-9).
[!*abc*...]	Match any character *not* enclosed as above.
~	Home directory of the current user.
~name	Home directory of user *name*.

~+	Current working directory (\$PWD).
~-	Previous working directory (\$OLDPWD).

With the extglob option on:

?(pattern)	Match zero or one instance of *pattern*.
*(pattern)	Match zero or more instances of *pattern*.
+(pattern)	Match one or more instances of *pattern*.
@(pattern)	Match exactly one instance of *pattern*.
!(pattern)	Match any strings that don't match *pattern*.

The *pattern* can be a sequence of patterns separated by |, meaning that the match applies to any of the patterns. This extended syntax resembles that available in egrep and awk.

With the globstar option on:

**	Match all files and zero or more subdirectories. When followed by a slash, only directories and subdirectories are matched.

Bash supports the POSIX [[=c=]] notation for matching characters that have the same weight, and [[.c.]] for specifying collating sequences. In addition, character classes, of the form [[:*class*:]], allow you to match the following classes of characters:

Class	Characters matched
alnum	Alphanumeric characters
alpha	Alphabetic characters
ascii	ASCII characters (not in POSIX)
blank	Space or Tab
cntrl	Control characters
digit	Decimal digits
graph	Nonspace characters

Class	Characters matched
lower	Lowercase characters
print	Printable characters
punct	Punctuation characters
space	Whitespace characters
upper	Uppercase characters
word	[[:word:]] is the same as [[:alnum:]_] (not in POSIX)
xdigit	Hexadecimal digits

Tip

Bash reads scripts one line at a time. It parses each line completely before beginning to execute any of the commands on the line. This has two implications:

- You cannot define an alias and then use it on the same line.
- You should place commands that affect parsing of the script on lines by themselves, before the parts of the script that are affected.

Similar concerns apply to functions; they are parsed all at once, so you cannot turn on the extglob option inside a function body expecting it to affect just that function. Thus, in order to use the extended pattern matching facilities, you should put this command on a line by itself at the beginning of your script:

```
shopt -s extglob    # enable extended shell patterns
```

Examples

`ls new*`	List new and new.1
`cat ch?`	Match ch9 but not ch10
`gvim [D-R]*`	Match files beginning with D through R
`pr !(*.o|core) | lpr`	Print non-object and non-core files

NOTE

On modern systems, ranges such as [D-R] are not portable; the system's locale may include more than just the uppercase letters from D to R in the range. However, see the globasciiranges shell option for a way to control this.

Brace Expansion

Bash has long supported brace expansion, based on a similar feature from the C shell. Unlike filename metacharacters, brace expansion is purely textual; the words created by brace expansion do not have to match existing files. There are two forms:

pre{X,Y[,Z...]}post
    Expands to preXpost, preYpost, and so on.

pre{start..end[..incr]}post
    start and *end* are either integers or single letters. *incr* is an integer. The shell expands this construct to the full range between *start* and *end*, increasing by *incr* if supplied.

The prefix and postfix texts are not required for either form. For numeric expansion, *start* or *end* or both may be prefixed with one or more leading zeros. The results of expansion are padded with zeros to the maximum of the widths of *start* and *end*. Bash ignores leading zeros on *incr*, always treating it as a decimal value.

Brace expansions may be nested, and the results are *not* sorted. Brace expansion is performed before other expansions, and the opening and closing braces must not be quoted for Bash to recognize them. Bash skips over command substitutions within brace expansions. To avoid conflict with parameter expansion, $\{$ cannot start a brace expansion.

Examples

```
# Expand textually; no sorting
$ echo hi{DDD,BBB,CCC,AAA}there
hiDDDthere hiBBBthere hiCCCthere hiAAAthere

# Expand, then match ch1, ch2, app1, app2
$ ls {ch,app}?

# Expands to mv info info.old
$ mv info{,.old}

# Simple numeric expansion
$ echo 1 to 10 is {1..10}
1 to 10 is 1 2 3 4 5 6 7 8 9 10

# Numeric expansion with increment
$ echo 1 to 10 by 2 is {1..10..2}
1 to 10 by 2 is 1 3 5 7 9

# Numeric expansion with zero padding
$ echo 1 to 10 with zeros is {01..10}
1 to 10 with zeros is 01 02 03 04 05 06 07 08 09 10
```

Escape Sequences

Bash recognizes and interprets special *escape sequences* in three different contexts:

- The $'...' quoted string
- Arguments to echo -e and printf %b
- Format strings for printf

The following table lists common escape sequences (those accepted in all contexts) as well as the unique escape sequences for each of the above contexts:

Sequence	Availability	Value
\a	All	ASCII BEL (visual or audible alert)
\b	All	Backspace
\c	echo -e, printf %b	Suppress the terminating newline (like echo -n) and do not print any following characters
\cX	$'...'	Control character X
\e	All	Escape
\E	All	Escape
\f	All	Formfeed
\n	All	Newline
\r	All	Carriage return
\t	All	Tab
\uHHHH	All	Unicode character HHHH
\UHHHHHHHH	All	Unicode character HHHHHHHH
\v	All	Vertical tab
\xHH	All	Hexadecimal value HH
\nnn	$'...', printf	Octal value nnn
\0nnn	echo -e, printf %b	Octal value nnn
\'	$'...'	Single quote
\"	$'...'	Double quote
\?	$'...'	Question mark
\\	All	Backslash

Additionally, the shell interprets a slightly overlapping set of escape sequences in the values of the PS0, PS1, PS2, and PS4 prompt strings. This is discussed in the section "Special Prompt Strings" on page 46.

Quoting

Quoting disables a character's special meaning and allows it to be used literally. The following table displays characters that have special meaning:

Character	Meaning
;	Command separator
&	Background execution
( )	Command grouping
|	Pipe
< > &	Redirection symbols
* ? [ ] ~ + - @ !	Filename metacharacters
" ' \	Used in quoting other characters
`	Command substitution
$	Variable substitution (or command or arithmetic substitution)
#	Start a comment that continues to the end of the line
space tab newline	Word separators

These characters can be used for quoting:

"..."

> Everything between " and " is taken literally, except for the following characters that keep their special meaning:

>> $ Variable (or command and arithmetic) substitution will occur.

>> `   Command substitution will occur.

>> "   This marks the end of the double quoted string.

'...'

> Everything between ' and ' is taken literally, except for another '. You cannot embed another ' within such a quoted string.

\   The character following a \ is taken literally. Use within "..." to escape ", $, and `. Often used to escape itself, spaces, or newlines.

$"..."

> Just like "...", except that locale translation is done.

$'...'

> Similar to '...', but the quoted text is processed for escape sequences as described in the section "Escape Sequences" on page 12.

Examples

```
$ echo 'Single quotes "protect" double quotes'
Single quotes "protect" double quotes
$ echo "Well, isn't that \"special\"?"
Well, isn't that "special"?
$ echo "You have `ls | wc -l` files in `pwd`"
You have       43 files in /home/bob
$ echo "The value of \$x is $x"
The value of $x is 100
$ echo $'A\tB'
A       B
```

Command Forms

cmd &	Execute cmd in background.
cmd1 ; cmd2	Command sequence; execute multiple cmds on the same line.
{ cmd1 ; cmd2 ; }	Execute commands as a group in the current shell.
(cmd1 ; cmd2)	Execute commands as a group in a subshell.
cmd1 | cmd2	Pipe; use output from cmd1 as input to cmd2.
cmd1 `cmd2`	Command substitution; use cmd2 output as arguments to cmd1.
cmd1 $(cmd2)	POSIX shell command substitution; nesting is allowed.
cmd $((expression))	POSIX shell arithmetic substitution. Use the numeric result of expression as a command-line argument to cmd.
cmd1 && cmd2	AND; execute cmd1 and then (if cmd1 succeeds) cmd2. This is a "short circuit" operation: cmd2 is never executed if cmd1 fails.
cmd1 || cmd2	OR; execute either cmd1 or (if cmd1 fails) cmd2. This is a "short circuit" operation; cmd2 is never executed if cmd1 succeeds.
! cmd	NOT; execute cmd, and produce a zero exit status if cmd exits with a nonzero status. Otherwise, produce a nonzero status when cmd exits with a zero status.

Examples

```
# Format in the background
$ nroff file > file.txt &

# Execute sequentially
$ cd; ls

# All output is redirected
```

```
$ (date; who; pwd) > logfile

# Sort file, page output, then print
$ sort file | pr -3 | lpr

# Edit files found by grep
$ gvim `grep -l ifdef *.cpp`

# Specify a list of files to search
$ egrep '(yes|no)' `cat list`

# POSIX version of previous
$ egrep '(yes|no)' $(cat list)

# Faster; not in POSIX
$ egrep '(yes|no)' $(< list)

# Print file if it contains the pattern
# Do so silently, by sending output and
# errors to /dev/null
$ grep XX file > /dev/null 2>&1 && lpr file

# Otherwise, echo an error message
$ grep XX file || echo "XX not found"
```

Redirection Forms

File descriptor	Name	Common abbreviation	Typical default
0	Standard input	stdin	Keyboard
1	Standard output	stdout	Screen
2	Standard error	stderr	Screen

The usual input source or output destination can be changed, as seen in the following sections.

Simple redirection

cmd > *file*

Send output of *cmd* to *file* (overwrite).

cmd >> *file*

> Send output of *cmd* to *file* (append).

cmd < *file*

> Take input for *cmd* from *file*.

cmd << *text*

> The contents of the shell script up to a line identical to *text* become the standard input for *cmd* (*text* can be stored in a shell variable). This command form is sometimes called a *here document*. Input is typed at the keyboard or in the shell program. Commands that typically use this syntax include cat, ex, and sed. (If <<- is used, leading tabs are stripped from the contents of the here document, and the tabs are ignored when comparing input with the end-of-input *text* marker.) If any part of *text* is quoted, the input is passed through verbatim. Otherwise, the contents are processed for variable, command, and arithmetic substitutions.

cmd <<< *word*

> Supply text of *word*, with trailing newline, as input to *cmd*. (This is known as a *here string*, from the free version of the rc shell; see the section "Resources" on page 133.)

cmd <> *file*

> Open *file* for reading *and* writing on the standard input. The contents are not destroyed.[1]

cmd >| *file*

> Send output of *cmd* to *file* (overwrite), even if the shell's noclobber option is set.

---

1 With <, the file is opened read-only, and writes on the file descriptor will fail. With <>, the file is opened read-write; it is up to the application to actually take advantage of this.

Redirection using file descriptors

cmd >&*n*

Send *cmd* output to file descriptor *n*.

cmd m>&*n*

Same as previous, except that output that would normally go to file descriptor *m* is sent to file descriptor *n* instead.

cmd >&-

Close standard output.

cmd <&*n*

Take input for *cmd* from file descriptor *n*.

cmd m<&*n*

Same as previous, except that input that would normally come from file descriptor *m* comes from file descriptor *n* instead.

cmd <&-

Close standard input.

cmd <&*n*-

Move file descriptor *n* to standard input by duplicating it and then closing the original.

cmd >&*n*-

Move file descriptor *n* to standard output by duplicating it and then closing the original.

Multiple redirection

cmd 2> *file*

Send standard error to *file*; standard output remains the same (e.g., the screen).

cmd > *file* 2>&1

Send both standard output and standard error to *file*.

cmd >& *file*

Same as previous.

cmd &> *file*
> Same as previous. Preferred form.

cmd &>> *file*
> Append both standard output and standard error to *file*.

cmd > *filea* 2> *fileb*
> Send standard output to file *filea* and standard error to file *fileb*.

cmd | tee *files*
> Send output of *cmd* to standard output (usually the terminal) and to *files*. See *tee*(1).

cmd 2>&1 | tee *files*
> Send standard output and error output of *cmd* through a pipe to **tee** to standard output (usually the terminal) and to *files*.

cmd |& tee *files*
> Same as previous.

Bash allows multidigit file descriptor numbers without any special syntax. Most other shells either require a special syntax or do not offer the feature at all.

NOTE

No space is allowed between file descriptors and a redirection symbol; spacing is optional in the other cases.

Process substitution

cmd <(*command*)
> Run *command* with its output connected to a named pipe or an open file in */dev/fd*, and place the file's name in the argument list of *cmd*. *cmd* may read the file to see the output of *command*.

---

cmd >(*command*)

> Run *command* with its input connected to a named pipe or an open file in */dev/fd*, and place the file's name in the argument list of *cmd*. Output written by *cmd* to the file is input to *command*.

Process substitution is available on systems that support either named pipes (FIFOs) or accessing open files via filenames in */dev/fd*. (This is true of all modern Unix systems.) It provides a way to create non-linear pipelines.

Process substitution is not available in POSIX mode shells.

Saving file descriptors in variables

Bash allows {*variablename*} instead of a file descriptor number in redirections. In such a case, the shell uses a file descriptor number greater than 9, and assigns the value to the named shell variable. *variablename* may name array elements and variables that are special to the shell. For example:

```
# Save file descriptor number
$ echo foo {foofd}> /tmp/xyzzy
foo
$ echo $foofd
11
```

This is most often used with redirections with **exec**, so that you can use the file descriptor later on in a script.

NOTE

Once you open a file descriptor this way, you are responsible for closing it. Bash will not close it for you.

Special filenames

Bash recognizes several special filenames in redirections. These are interpreted internally by Bash only if they are not present on your system:

/dev/stdin
> A duplicate of file descriptor 0.

/dev/stdout
> A duplicate of file descriptor 1.

/dev/stderr
> A duplicate of file descriptor 2.

/dev/fd/<n>
> A duplicate of file descriptor *<n>*.

/dev/tcp/<host>/<port>
> Bash opens a TCP connection to *<host>*, which is either a hostname or IP address, on port *<port>* and uses the file descriptor in the redirection.

/dev/udp/<host>/<port>
> Bash opens a UDP connection to *<host>*, which is either a hostname or IP address, on port *<port>* and uses the file descriptor in the redirection.

Examples

```
# Copy part1 to book
$ cat part1 > book

# Append part2 and part3
$ cat part2 part3 >> book

# Send report to the big boss
$ mail tim < report

# Here document is sed's input
$ sed 's/^/XX /g' << END_ARCHIVE
> This is often how a shell archive is "wrapped",
> bundling text for distribution.  You would normally
```

```
> run sed from a shell program, not from
> the command line.
> END_ARCHIVE
XX This is often how a shell archive is "wrapped",
XX bundling text for distribution.  You would normally
XX run sed from a shell program, not from
XX the command line.
```

To redirect standard output to standard error:

```
$ echo "Usage error: see administrator" 1>&2
```

The following command sends output (files found) to *filelist*, and error messages (inaccessible files) to *no_access*:

```
$ find / -print > filelist 2> no_access
```

The following sorts two files and presents the differences between the results using the `diff` command:

```
$ diff -u <(sort file1) <(sort file2) | less
```

Functions

A shell *function* is a grouping of commands within a shell script. Shell functions let you modularize your program by dividing it up into separate tasks. This way, the code for each task is not repeated every time you need to perform the task. The POSIX shell syntax for defining a function follows the Bourne shell:

```
name () {
    function body's code comes here
} [redirections]
```

Functions are invoked in the same way as regular shell built-in commands or external commands. The command-line parameters $1, $2, and so on receive the function's arguments, temporarily hiding the global values of $1, $2, and so on. $0 remains the name of the full script. For example:

```
# fatal --- print an error message and die:

fatal () {
    # Messages go to standard error.
    echo "$0: fatal error:" "$@" >&2
    exit 1
}
…
if [ $# = 0 ]      # not enough arguments
then
    fatal not enough arguments
fi
```

A function may use the return command to return an exit status to the calling shell program.

Per the POSIX standard, any *redirections* given with the function definition are evaluated when the function executes, not when it is defined.

Bash allows you to define functions using a slightly different syntax, as follows:

```
function name [()] { body } [redirections]
```

When using the function keyword, the parentheses following the function name are optional.

Functions whose names do not include = or / may be exported into the environment with export -f; see the entry for export on page 92.

Functions share traps (see the entry for trap on page 125) with the "parent" shell as described in the following table:

Trap type	Shared/not shared
Signal-based traps	Shared until the function redefines the trap
DEBUG	Not shared unless function tracing is enabled (set -T or set -o functrace). If not enabled a DEBUG trap created by a function call remains in place when the function returns

Trap type	Shared/not shared
ERR	Not shared unless error tracing is enabled (`set -E` or `set -o errtrace`)
EXIT	Shared until the function redefines the trap
RETURN	Not shared unless function tracing is enabled (`set -T` or `set -o functrace`)

Functions may have local variables, and they may be recursive. Unlike the Korn shell, the syntax used to define a function is irrelevant.

Function names do not have to be valid shell identifiers (just as external commands are not required to have names that are valid shell identifiers). This does not apply to POSIX mode shells, however. Additionally, POSIX mode shells disallow defining functions with the same name as a POSIX special built-in command. Doing so is an error in interactive shells; it is fatal in noninteractive shells.

Bash uses a *dynamic scoping* model, whereby variables declared with `local` are visible inside that function *and* in other functions that it calls. This is different from many other Bourne-style shells.

Tip

Be careful *not* to use `exit` from within a function unless you really wish to terminate the entire program.

Variables

This section describes the following:

- Variable assignment
- Variable substitution
- Indirect variables (namerefs)
- Built-in shell variables

- Other shell variables
- Arrays
- Special prompt strings

Variable Assignment

Variable names consist of any number of letters, digits, or underscores. Upper- and lowercase letters are distinct, and names may not start with a digit. Variables are assigned values using the = operator. There must *not* be any whitespace between the variable name and the value. You can make multiple assignments on the same line by separating each one with whitespace:

```
firstname=Arnold lastname=Robbins numkids=4 numpets=1
```

By convention, names for variables used or set by the shell have all uppercase letters; however, you can use uppercase names in your scripts if you use a name that isn't special to the shell.

By default, the shell treats variable values as strings, even if the value of the string is all digits. However, when a value is assigned to an integer variable (created via declare -i), Bash evaluates the righthand side of the assignment as an expression (see the section "Arithmetic Expressions" on page 47). For example:

```
$ i=5+3 ; echo $i
5+3
$ declare -i jj ; jj=5+3 ; echo $jj
8
```

The += operator allows you to add or append the righthand side of the assignment to an existing value. Integer variables treat the righthand side as an expression, which is evaluated and added to the value. Arrays add the new elements to the array (see the section "Arrays" on page 44). For example:

```
$ name=Arnold                    String variable
$ name+=" Robbins" ; echo $name
```

```
Arnold Robbins
$ declare -i jj ; jj=3+5      Integer variable
$ echo $jj
8
$ jj+=2+4 ; echo $jj
14
$ pets=(blacky rusty)         Array variable
$ echo ${pets[*]}
blacky rusty
$ pets+=(raincloud sophie)
$ echo ${pets[*]}
blacky rusty raincloud sophie
```

Variable Substitution

No spaces should be used in the following expressions. The colon (:) is optional; if it's included, *var* must be nonnull as well as set. The variable substitution forms honor the value of the shell nocasematch option.

In noninteractive shells with set -u enabled, using an unset variable with the #, ##, %, %%, //, /#, /%, ^, ^^, ,, and ,, substitutions causes the shell to exit.

Consider single-quoted text in a variable substitution, such as ${var:=a'special-text'b}. Here, special-text is recognized as being quoted. However, in POSIX mode, when a variable substitution occurs inside double quotes, such single quotes do not define a new, nested quoting context. There are exceptions: single quotes do provide quoting when used with the #, ##, %, %%, //, /#, /%, ^, ^^, ,, and ,, substitutions.

var=value ...	Set each variable *var* to a *value*.
${*var*}	Use value of *var*; braces are optional if *var* is separated from the following text. They are required for array variables.
${*var*:-*value*}	Use *var* if set; otherwise, use *value*.

`${var:=value}`	Use *var* if set; otherwise, use *value* and assign *value* to *var*.
`${var:?value}`	Use *var* if set; otherwise, print *value* and exit (if not interactive). If *value* isn't supplied, print the phrase `parameter null or not set` to stderr.
`${var:+value}`	Use *value* if *var* is set; otherwise, use nothing.
`${#var}`	Use the length of *var*.
`${#*}, ${#@}`	Use the number of positional parameters.
`${var#pattern}`	Use value of *var* after removing text matching *pattern* from the left. Remove the shortest matching piece.
`${var##pattern}`	Same as *#pattern*, but remove the longest matching piece.
`${var%pattern}`	Use value of *var* after removing text matching *pattern* from the right. Remove the shortest matching piece.
`${var%%pattern}`	Same as *%pattern*, but remove the longest matching piece.
`${var^pattern}`	Convert the case of *var* to uppercase. The *pattern* is evaluated as for filename matching. If the first letter of *var*'s value matches the pattern, it is converted to uppercase. *var* can be * or @, in which case the positional parameters are modified. *var* can also be an array subscripted by * or @, in which case the substitution is applied to all the elements of the array.
`${var^^pattern}`	Same as *^pattern*, but apply the match to every letter in the string.
`${var,pattern}`	Same as *^pattern*, but convert matching characters to lowercase. Applies only to the first character in the string.
`${var,,pattern}`	Same as *,pattern*, but apply the match to every letter in the string.

`${var@a}`	Use the flag values (as for `declare`) representing *var*'s attributes. *var* may be an array subscripted with @ or *, in which case the transform applies to all the elements.
`${var@A}`	A string in the form of a command or assignment statement that if evaluated recreates *var* and its attributes. *var* may be an array subscripted with @ or *, in which case the transform applies to all the elements.
`${var@E}`	The value of *var* with `$'...'` escape sequences evaluated (see the section "Escape Sequences" on page 12). *var* may be an array subscripted with @ or *, in which case the transform applies to all the elements.
`${var@P}`	The value of *var* with prompt string escape sequences evaluated (see the section "Special Prompt Strings" on page 46). *var* may be an array subscripted with @ or *, in which case the transform applies to all the elements.
`${var@Q}`	The value of *var* quoted in a way that allows entering the values as input. *var* may be an array subscripted with @ or *, in which case the transform applies to all the elements.
`${!prefix*}`, `${!prefix@}`	List of variables whose names begin with *prefix*.
`${var:pos}`, `${var:pos:len}`	Starting at position *pos* (0-based) in variable *var*, extract *len* characters, or extract rest of string if no *len*. *pos* and *len* may be arithmetic expressions. A negative *len* counts from the end of the string. When *var* is * or @, the expansion is performed upon the positional parameters. If *pos* is zero, then $0 is included in the resulting list. Similarly, *var* can be an array indexed by * or @.
`${var/pat/repl}`	Use value of *var*, with first match of *pat* replaced with *repl*.
`${var/pat}`	Use value of *var*, with first match of *pat* deleted.

`${var//pat/repl}`	Use value of *var*, with every match of *pat* replaced with *repl*.
`${var/#pat/repl}`	Use value of *var*, with match of *pat* replaced with *repl*. Match must occur at the beginning of the value.
`${var/%pat/repl}`	Use value of *var*, with match of *pat* replaced with *repl*. Match must occur at the end of the value.
`${!var}`	Use value of *var* as name of variable whose value should be used (indirect reference).

Examples

```
$ u=up d=down blank=          Assign values to three variables
                              (last is null)
$ echo ${u}root               Braces are needed here
uproot
$ echo ${u-$d}                Display value of u or d; u is set,
up                            so print it
$ echo ${tmp-`date`}          If tmp not set, execute date
Tue Feb  2 22:52:57 EST 2016
$ echo ${blank="no data"}     blank is set, so it is printed
                              (blank line)
$ echo ${blank:="no data"}    blank is set but null, print string
no data
$ echo $blank                 blank now has a new value
no data

# Take the current directory name and remove the
# longest character string ending with /, which
# removes the leading pathname and leaves the tail
$ tail=${PWD##*/}

# Use a famous word
$ word=supercalifragilisticexpialidocious

# Modify the case of the first character
$ echo ${word^[r-t]}
Supercalifragilisticexpialidocious
```

```
# Modify the case of all matching characters
$ echo ${word^^[r-t]}
SupeRcalifRagiliSTicexpialidociouS
```

Indirect Variables (namerefs)

Indirect variables, or *namerefs*, are variables that name a second variable. All actions (references, assignments, and attribute changes) applied to the nameref are done to the variable named by the nameref's value. Namerefs are created using declare -n, removed using unset -n, and tested for with test -R. For example:

`$ greeting="hello, world"`	*Regular variable assignment*
`$ declare -n message=greeting`	*Declare the nameref*
`$ echo $message`	*Access through it*
`hello, world`	*Value is $greeting*
`$ message="bye now"`	*Assign through the nameref*
`$ echo $greeting`	*Demonstrate the change*
`bye now`	

Bash also provides a special syntax that lets one variable indirectly reference another, but assignments with this syntax are not possible:

`$ text=greeting`	*Regular variable assignment*
`$ echo ${!text}`	*Use the alias*
`bye now`	

When a nameref is used as the control variable in a for loop, the loop terms are treated as variable names and the nameref refers to each in turn:

`$ declare -n nr`	*Set up nameref*
`$ i=1`	*A simple counter*
`$ for nr in v1 v2 v3`	*Start a loop*
`> do`	
`>     nr=$((i++))`	*Each variable gets a unique value*
`> done`	
`$ echo $v1 $v2 $v3`	*Show results*
`1 2 3`	

Converting an existing variable into a nameref disables the -c, -i, -l and -u attributes (see the entry for declare on page 85).

Built-In Shell Variables

The shell automatically sets built-in variables; they are typically used inside shell scripts. Built-in variables can use the variable substitution patterns shown previously. Note that the $ is not actually part of the variable name, although the variable is always referenced this way. The following are available in any Bourne-compatible shell:

$#   Number of command-line arguments.

$-   Options currently in effect (supplied on command line or to set). The shell sets some options automatically.

$?   Exit value of last executed command.

$$ Process number of the shell.

$!   Process number of last background command.

$0   First word; that is, the command name. This will have the full pathname if the command was found via a PATH search.

$n   Individual arguments on the command line (positional parameters). The Bourne shell allows only nine parameters to be referenced directly (n = 1–9); Bash allows n to be greater than 9 if specified as ${n}.

$*, $@ All arguments on the command line ($1 $2 ...).

"$*"   All arguments on the command line as one string ("$1 $2..."). The values are separated by the first character in $IFS.

"$@"   All arguments on the command line, individually quoted ("$1" "$2" ...).

Bash automatically sets the following additional variables:[2]

$_	Temporary variable; initialized to the pathname of the script or program being executed. Later, stores the last argument of the previous command. Also stores the name of the matching MAIL file during mail checks.
BASH	The full pathname used to invoke this instance of Bash.
BASHOPTS	A read-only, colon-separated list of shell options that are currently enabled. Each item in the list is a valid option for shopt -s. If this variable exists in the environment when Bash starts up, it sets the indicated options before executing any startup files.
BASHPID	The process ID of the current Bash process. In some cases, this can differ from $$.
BASH_ALIASES	Associative array variable. Each element holds an alias defined with the alias command. Adding an element to this array creates a new alias.
BASH_ARGC	Array variable. Each element holds the number of arguments for the corresponding function or dot-script invocation. Set only in extended debug mode, with shopt -s extdebug. It cannot be unset.

---

2 Not all variables are always set. For example, the COMP* variables only have values while programmable completion functions are running.

BASH_ARGV	An array variable similar to BASH_ARGC. Each element is one of the arguments passed to a function or dot-script. It functions as a stack, with values being pushed on at each call. Thus, the last element is the last argument to the most recent function or script invocation. Set only in extended debug mode, with shopt -s extdebug. It cannot be unset.
BASH_CMDS	Associative array variable. Each element refers to a command in the internal hash table maintained by the hash command. The index is the command name and the value is the full path to the command. Adding an element to this array adds a command to the hash table.
BASH_COMMAND	The command currently executing or about to be executed. Inside a trap handler, it is the command running when the trap was invoked.
BASH_EXECUTION_STRING	The string argument passed to the -c option.
BASH_LINENO	Array variable, corresponding to BASH_SOURCE and FUNCNAME. For any given function number i (starting at zero), ${FUNCNAME[i]} was invoked in file ${BASH_SOURCE[i]} on line ${BASH_LINENO[i]}. The information is stored with the most recent function invocation first. It cannot be unset.
BASH_REMATCH	Array variable, assigned by the =~ operator of the [[ ]] construct. Index zero is the text that matched the entire pattern. The other indices are the text matched by parenthesized subexpressions. This variable is read-only.
BASH_SOURCE	Array variable, containing source filenames. Each element corresponds to those in FUNCNAME and BASH_LINENO. It cannot be unset.

BASH_SUBSHELL	This variable is incremented by one each time a subshell or subshell environment is created.
BASH_VERSINFO[0]	The major version number, or release, of Bash.
BASH_VERSINFO[1]	The minor version number, or version, of Bash.
BASH_VERSINFO[2]	The patch level.
BASH_VERSINFO[3]	The build version.
BASH_VERSINFO[4]	The release status.
BASH_VERSINFO[5]	The machine type; same value as in $MACHTYPE.
BASH_VERSION	A string describing the version of Bash.
COMP_CWORD	For programmable completion. Index into COMP_WORDS, indicating the current cursor position.
COMP_KEY	For programmable completion. The key, or final key in a sequence, that caused the invocation of the current completion function.
COMP_LINE	For programmable completion. The current command line.
COMP_POINT	For programmable completion. The position of the cursor as a character index in $COMP_LINE.
COMP_TYPE	For programmable completion. A character describing the type of programmable completion. The character is one of Tab for normal completion, ? for a completions list after two Tabs, ! for the list of alternatives on partial word completion, @ for completions if the word is modified, or % for menu completion.
COMP_WORDBREAKS	For programmable completion. The characters that the *readline* library treats as word separators when doing word completion.

COMP_WORDS	For programmable completion. Array variable containing the individual words on the command line.
COPROC	Array variable that holds the file descriptors used for communicating with an unnamed coprocess. For more information, see the section "Coprocesses" on page 68.
DIRSTACK	Array variable, containing the contents of the directory stack as displayed by dirs. Changing existing elements modifies the stack, but only pushd and popd can add or remove elements from the stack.
EUID	Read-only variable with the numeric effective UID of the current user.
FUNCNAME	Array variable, containing function names. Each element corresponds to those in BASH_SOURCE and BASH_LINENO.
FUNCNEST	A value greater than zero defines the maximum function call nesting level. When exceeded, abort the current command.
GROUPS	Array variable, containing the list of numeric group IDs in which the current user is a member.
HISTCMD	The history number of the current command.
HOSTNAME	The name of the current host.
HOSTTYPE	A string that describes the host system.
LINENO	Current line number within the script or function.
MACHTYPE	A string that describes the host system in the GNU *cpu-company-system* format.

MAPFILE	Default array for the `mapfile` and `readarray` commands. See the entry for `mapfile` on page 105 for more information.
OLDPWD	Previous working directory (set by `cd`, or inherited from the environment if it names a directory).
OPTARG	Value of argument to last option processed by `getopts`.
OPTIND	Numerical index of OPTARG.
OSTYPE	A string that describes the operating system.
PIPESTATUS	Array variable, containing the exit statuses of the commands in the most recent foreground pipeline. Note that a pipeline can contain only a single command.
PPID	Process number of this shell's parent.
PWD	Current working directory (set by `cd`).
RANDOM[=*n*]	Generate a new random number with each reference; start with integer *n*, if given.
READLINE_LINE	For use with `bind -x`. The contents of the editing buffer are available in this variable.
READLINE_POINT	For use with `bind -x`. The index in $READLINE_LINE of the insertion point.
REPLY	Default reply; used by `select` and `read`.
SECONDS[=*n*]	Number of seconds since the shell was started, or, if *n* is given, number of seconds since the assignment + *n*.
SHELLOPTS	A read-only, colon-separated list of shell options (for `set -o`). If set in the environment at startup, Bash enables each option present in the list before reading any startup files.

SHLVL	Incremented by one every time a new Bash starts up.
UID	Read-only variable with the numeric real UID of the current user.

Many of these variables provide support for either programmable completion (see the section "Programmable Completion" on page 54) or for the Bash Debugger (see *http://bashdb.source forge.net*).

Other Shell Variables

The following variables are not automatically set by the shell, although many of them can influence the shell's behavior. You typically set them in your *.bash_profile* or *.profile* file, where you can define them to suit your needs. Variables can be assigned values by issuing commands of the form:

```
variable=value
```

This list includes the type of value expected when defining these variables:

BASH_COMPAT	If set to a decimal or integer value (such as 4.3 or 43) that corresponds to a supported shell compatibility level, enables that compatibility level (e.g., 4.3 and 43 correspond to shopt -s compat43). If unset or set to the empty string, the compatibility is set to that of the current shell. The shopt command does not change this variable. This variable can be inherited from the environment.
BASH_ENV	If set at startup, names a file to be processed for initialization commands. The value undergoes parameter expansion, command substitution, and arithmetic expansion before being interpreted as a filename.

BASH_LOADABLES_PATH	One or more pathnames, delimited by colons, in which to search for dynamically loadable built-in commands specified by `enable`.
BASH_XTRACEFD=*n*	File descriptor to which Bash writes trace output (from `set -x`).
CDPATH=*dirs*	Directories searched by `cd`; allows shortcuts in changing directories; unset by default.
CHILD_MAX=*n*	Set the maximum number of child processes for which the shell will remember exit statuses. The maximum is 8192; the minimum is system-dependent.
COLUMNS=*n*	Screen's column width; used in line edit modes and `select` lists. Defaults to current terminal width.
COMPREPLY=(*words ...*)	Array variable from which Bash reads the possible completions generated by a completion function.
EMACS	If the value starts with t, Bash assumes it's running in an Emacs buffer and disables line editing.
ENV=*file*	Name of script that is executed at startup in POSIX mode or when Bash is invoked as */bin/sh*; useful for storing alias and function definitions. For example, ENV=$HOME/.shellrc.
EXECIGNORE=*patlist*	Colon-separated list of glob patterns describing the set of filenames to ignore when searching for executable files. Useful for ignoring shared library files which have execute permission. The value of the `extglob` shell option is honored.

FCEDIT=*file*	Editor used by fc command. The default is /bin/ed when Bash is in POSIX mode. Otherwise, the default is $EDITOR if set, vi if unset.
FIGNORE=*patlist*	Colon-separated list of suffixes describing the set of filenames to ignore when doing filename completion with the *readline* library.
GLOBIGNORE=*patlist*	Colon-separated list of patterns describing the set of filenames to ignore during pattern matching. The value of the nocasematch and extglob shell options are honored.
HISTCONTROL=*list*	Colon-separated list of values controlling how commands are saved in the history file. Recognized values are ignoredups, ignorespace, ignoreboth, and erasedups.
HISTFILE=*file*	File in which to store command history. Default value is ~/.bash_history.
HISTFILESIZE=*n*	Number of lines to be kept in the history file. This may be different from the number of commands. If zero, no commands are stored. If negative or nonnumeric, there is no limit. Default is 500.
HISTIGNORE=*list*	A colon-separated list of patterns that must match the entire command line. Matching lines are *not* saved in the history file. An unescaped & in a pattern matches the previous history line. The value of the extglob shell option is honored.
HISTSIZE=*n*	Number of history commands to be kept in the history list. If zero, no commands are stored. If negative or nonnumeric, there is no limit. Default is 500.

HISTTIMEFORMAT=*string*	A format string for *strftime*(3) to use for printing timestamps along with commands from the `history` command. If set (even if null), Bash saves timestamps in the history file along with the commands.
HOME=*dir*	Home directory; set by `login` (from the */etc/passwd* file).
HOSTFILE=*file*	Name of a file in the same format as */etc/hosts* that Bash should use to find hostnames for hostname completion.
IFS='*chars*'	Input field separators; default is space, Tab, and newline.
IGNOREEOF=*n*	Numeric value indicating how many successive EOF characters must be typed before Bash exits. If null or nonnumeric value, default is 10. Applies only to interactive shells.
INPUTRC=*file*	Initialization file for the *readline* library. This overrides the default value of *~/.inputrc*.
LANG=*locale*	Default value for locale; used if no LC_* variables are set.
LC_ALL=*locale*	Current locale; overrides LANG and the other LC_* variables.
LC_COLLATE=*locale*	Locale to use for character collation (sorting order).
LC_CTYPE=*locale*	Locale to use for character class functions. (See the section "Filename Metacharacters" on page 8.)
LC_MESSAGES=*locale*	Locale to use for translating $"..." strings.
LC_NUMERIC=*locale*	Locale to use for the decimal-point character.
LC_TIME=*locale*	Locale to use for date and time formats.
LINES=*n*	Screen's height; used for `select` lists. Defaults to current terminal height.

MAIL=*file*	Default file to check for incoming mail; set by login.
MAILCHECK=*n*	Number of seconds between mail checks; default is 60 (one minute).
MAILPATH=*files*	One or more files, delimited by colons, to check for incoming mail. Along with each file, you may supply an optional message that the shell prints when the file increases in size. Messages are separated from the filename by a ? character, and You have mail in $_ is the default message. $_ is replaced with the name of the file. For example, you might have MAILPATH="$MAIL?Candy gram!:/etc/motd?New Login Mes sage"
OPTERR=*n*	When set to 1 (the default value), Bash prints error messages from the built-in getopts command.
PATH=*dirlist*	One or more pathnames, delimited by colons, in which to search for commands to execute. The compiled-in default is /usr/local/bin:/usr/local/sbin:/usr/bin:/usr/sbin:/bin:/sbin:.. The default for many systems is /bin:/usr/bin.
POSIXLY_CORRECT=*string*	When set at startup or while running, Bash enters POSIX mode, disabling behavior and modifying features that conflict with the POSIX standard.
PROMPT_COMMAND=*command*	If set, Bash executes this command each time before printing the primary prompt.

`PROMPT_DIRTRIM=n`	Indicates how many trailing directory components to retain for the `\w` or `\W` special prompt strings (see the section "Special Prompt Strings" on page 46). Elided components are replaced with an ellipsis.
`PS0=string`	String printed by interactive shells after reading a command but before executing it.
`PS1=string`	Primary prompt string; default is `'\s-\v\$ '`.
`PS2=string`	Secondary prompt (used in multiline commands); default is >.
`PS3=string`	Prompt string in `select` loops; default is #?.
`PS4=string`	Prompt string for execution trace (`bash -x` or `set -x`); default is +. Shells running as root do not inherit this variable from the environment.
`SHELL=file`	Name of user's default shell (e.g., */bin/sh*). Bash sets this if it's not in the environment at startup.
`TERM=string`	Terminal type.
`TIMEFORMAT=string`	A format string for the output from the `time` keyword. See the *bash*(1) manual page for details.
`TMOUT=n`	If no command is typed after *n* seconds, exit the shell. Also affects the `read` command and the `select` loop.
`TMPDIR=directory`	Place temporary files created and used by the shell in *directory*.

`auto_resume=list`	Enable the use of simple strings for resuming stopped jobs. With a value of `exact`, the string must match a command name exactly. With a value of `substring`, it can match a substring of the command name.
`histchars=chars`	Two or three characters that control Bash's `csh`-style history expansion. The first character signals a history event, the second is the "quick substitution" character, and the third indicates the start of a comment. The default value is `!^#`. See the section "C-Shell–Style History" on page 51.

Arrays

Bash provides two kinds of arrays: *indexed arrays*, where the indices are integers zero and above, and *associative arrays*, where the indices are strings.

Indexed arrays

Bash supports one-dimensional arrays. The first element is numbered zero. Bash has no limit on the number of elements. Arrays are initialized with a special form of assignment:

```
message=(hi there how are you today)
```

where the specified values become elements of the array. Individual elements may also be assigned:

```
message[0]=hi          # This is the hard way
message[1]=there
message[2]=how
message[3]=are
message[4]=you
message[5]=today
```

Declaring indexed arrays is not required. Any valid reference to a subscripted variable can create an array.

When referencing arrays, use the ${...} syntax. This isn't needed when referencing arrays inside ((...)) (the form of let that does automatic quoting). Note that [and] are typed literally (i.e., they don't stand for optional syntax).

Negative subscripts count from the last index plus one:

```
$ a=(0 1 2 3 4 5 6 7 8)        Create an indexed array
$ echo ${a[4]}                 Use a positive index
4
$ echo ${a[-2]}                Use index: 8 + 1 − 2 = 7
7
```

Array substitutions

The variable substitutions for arrays and array elements are as follows:

${name[i]}	Use element *i* of array *name*; *i* can be any arithmetic expression as described in the section "Arithmetic Expressions" on page 47
${name}	Use element 0 of array *name*
${name[*]}, ${name[@]}	Use all elements of array *name*
${#name[*]}, ${#name[@]}	Use the number of elements in array *name*

Associative arrays

Bash provides associative arrays, where the indices are strings instead of numbers (as in awk). In this case, [and] act like double quotes. Associative arrays must be declared by using the -A option to the declare, local, and readonly commands. A special syntax allows assigning to multiple elements at once:

```
data=([joe]=30 [mary]=25)      Associative array assignment
message=([0]=hi [2]=there)     Indexed array assignment
```

Use ${data[joe]} and ${data[mary]} to retrieve the values.

The special expansions for retrieving all the indices of an associative array work just as they do for indexed arrays.

Special Prompt Strings

Bash processes the values of PS0, PS1, PS2, and PS4 for the following special escape sequences:

\a	An ASCII BEL character (octal 07).
\A	The current time in 24-hour HH:MM format.
\d	The date in "weekday month day" format.
\D{*format*}	The date as specified by the *strftime*(3) format *format*. The braces are required.
\e	An ASCII Escape character (octal 033).
\h	The hostname, up to the first period.
\H	The full hostname.
\j	The current number of jobs.
\l	The basename of the shell's terminal device.
\n	A newline character.
\r	A carriage return character.
\s	The name of the shell (basename of $0).
\t	The current time in 24-hour HH:MM:SS format.
\T	The current time in 12-hour HH:MM:SS format.
\u	The current user's username.
\v	The version of Bash.
\V	The release (version plus patchlevel) of Bash.
\w	The current directory, with $HOME abbreviated as ~. See also the description of the PROMPT_DIRTRIM variable.
\W	The basename of the current directory, with $HOME abbreviated as ~. See also the description of the PROMPT_DIRTRIM variable.

`\!`	The history number of this command (stored in the history).
`\#`	The command number of this command (count of commands executed by the current shell).
`\$`	If the effective UID is 0, a #; otherwise, a $.
`\@`	The current time in 12-hour a.m./p.m. format.
`\nnn`	The character represented by octal value *nnn*.
`\\`	A literal backslash.
`\[`	Start a sequence of nonprinting characters, such as for highlighting or changing colors in a terminal emulator.
`\]`	End a sequence of nonprinting characters.

The `PS0`, `PS1`, `PS2`, and `PS4` variables undergo substitution for escape sequences, variable substitution, command substitution, and arithmetic substitution. The escape sequences are processed first, and then, if the `promptvars` shell option is enabled via the `shopt` command (the default), the substitutions are performed.

In POSIX mode, things work differently. The values of `PS1` and `PS2` undergo parameter expansion, ! is replaced with the history number of the current command, and !! is replaced with a literal exclamation point.

Arithmetic Expressions

The `let` command performs integer arithmetic. The shell provides a way to substitute arithmetic values (for use as command arguments or in variables); base conversion is also possible:

`$(( expr ))`	Use the value of the enclosed arithmetic expression. Bash attempts to parse `$((...))` as an arithmetic expression before attempting to parse it as a nested command substitution.
`B#n`	Interpret integer *n* in numeric base *B*. For example, `8#100` specifies the octal equivalent of decimal 64.

Operators

The shell uses the following arithmetic operators in decreasing order of precedence (most are from the C programming language):

Operator	Description
++ --	Auto-increment and auto-decrement, both prefix and postfix
+ -	Unary plus and minus
! ~	Logical negation and binary inversion (one's complement)
**	Exponentiation
* / %	Multiplication, division, modulus (remainder)
+ -	Addition, subtraction
<< >>	Bitwise left shift, bitwise right shift
< <= > >=	Less than, less than or equal to, greater than, greater than or equal to
== !=	Equality, inequality (both evaluated left to right)
&	Bitwise AND
^	Bitwise exclusive OR
|	Bitwise OR
&&	Logical AND (short circuit)
||	Logical OR (short circuit)
? :	Inline conditional evaluation
= += -=	
*= /= %=	
<<= >>=	Assignment
&= ^= |=	
,	Sequential expression evaluation

Notes

Because `let` and `((...))` are built in to the shell, they have access to variable values. It is not necessary to precede a variable's name with a dollar sign in order to retrieve its value (doing so does work, of course).

The exit status of `let` is confusing. It's zero (success) for a non-zero mathematical result, and non-zero (failure) for a zero mathematical result.

Examples

```
let "count=0" "i = i + 1"      Assign values to i and count
let "num % 2"                  Exit successfully if num is odd
(( percent <= 0 &&             Test the range of a value
   percent <= 100 ))
a=5 b=2                        Set some values
echo $(("a" + "b"))            Variables may be double-quoted
```

See the entry for `let` on page 104 for more information and examples.

Command History

The shell lets you display or modify previous commands. Using the `history` command, you can manage the list of commands kept in the shell's history; see the entry for `history` on page 100 for more information. All shells for which history is enabled (with `set -o history`) save their history, not just interactive shells.

This section focuses on the facilities for editing stored commands. Commands in the history list can be modified using:

- Line-edit mode
- The `fc` command
- C-shell–style history

Line-Edit Mode

Line-edit mode emulates many features of the vi and Emacs editors. The history list is treated like a file. When the editor is invoked, you type editing keystrokes to move to the command line you want to execute. You can also change the line before executing it. When you're ready to issue the command, press the Enter key.

Emacs editing mode is the default. To control command-line editing, you must use either set -o vi or set -o emacs; Bash does not use variables to specify the editor.

Note that the vi editing mode starts in input mode; to type a vi command, press the Escape key first.

Common editing keystrokes

vi	Emacs	Result
k	CTRL-p	Get previous command
j	CTRL-n	Get next command
/string	CTRL-r string	Get previous command containing string
h	CTRL-b	Move back one character
l	CTRL-f	Move forward one character
b	ESC-b	Move back one word
w	ESC-f	Move forward one word
X	DEL	Delete previous character
x	CTRL-d	Delete character under cursor
dw	ESC-d	Delete word forward
db	ESC-h	Delete word backward
xp	CTRL-t	Transpose two characters

Both editing modes allow you to use the cursor keys to move around within the saved history.

The fc Command

fc stands for either "find command" or "fix command,"
because it does both jobs. Use fc -l to list history commands
and fc -e to edit them. See the entry for fc on page 93 for
more information.

Examples

$ **history**	*List the last 16 commands*
$ **fc -l 20 30**	*List commands 20 through 30*
$ **fc -l -5**	*List the last 5 commands*
$ **fc -l cat**	*List all commands since the last cat*
$ **fc -l 50**	*List all commands since command 50*
$ **fc -ln 5 > doit**	*Save command 5 to file doit*
$ **fc -e vi 5 20**	*Edit commands 5 through 20 using vi*
$ **fc -e emacs**	*Edit previous command using Emacs*

Tip

Interactive line-editing is easier to use than fc, because you can
move up and down in the saved command history using your
favorite editor commands (as long as your favorite editor is
either vi or Emacs!). You may also use the Up and Down arrow
keys to traverse the command history.

C-Shell–Style History

Besides the interactive editing features and POSIX fc command, Bash supports a command-line editing mode similar to
that of the Berkeley C shell (csh). It can be disabled using set
+H. Many users prefer the interactive editing features, but for
those whose "finger habits" are still those of csh, this feature
comes in handy.

In POSIX mode, history expansion does not occur inside double quotes. It is always inhibited inside single quotes.

In Bash 5.0, set +H will become the default.

Event designators

Event designators mark a command-line word as a history substitution:

Command	Description
!	Begin a history substitution
!!	Previous command
!n	Command number *n* in history list
!-n	*n* th command back from current command
!string	Most recent command that starts with *string*
!?string[?]	Most recent command that contains *string*
#	Current command line up to this point (fairly useless)
^old^new^	Quick substitution; change string *old* to *new* in previous command, and execute modified command

Word substitution

Word specifiers allow you to retrieve individual words from previous command lines. They follow an initial event specifier, separated by a colon. The colon is optional if followed by any of the following: ^, $, *, -, or %.

Specifier	Description
:0	Command name
:n	Argument number *n*
^	First argument
$	Last argument
%	Argument matched by a !?*string*? search
:n-m	Arguments *n* through *m*
-m	Words 0 through *m*; same as :0-*m*
:n-	Arguments *n* through next-to-last

Specifier	Description
:n*	Arguments *n* through last; same as *n*-$
*	All arguments; same as ^-$ or 1-$

History modifiers

There are several ways to modify command and word substitutions. The printing, substitution, and quoting modifiers are shown in the following table:

Modifier	Description
:p	Display command, but don't execute.
:s/*old*/*new*	Substitute string *new* for *old*, first instance only.
:gs/*old*/*new*	Substitute string *new* for *old*, all instances.
:as/*old*/*new*	Same as :gs.
:Gs/*old*/*new*	Like :gs, but apply the substitution to all the words in the command line.
:&	Repeat previous substitution (:s or ^ command), first instance only.
:g&	Repeat previous substitution, all instances.
:q	Quote a word list.
:x	Quote separate words.

The truncation modifiers are shown in the following table:

Modifier	Description
:r	Extract the first available pathname root (the portion before the last period).
:e	Extract the first available pathname extension (the portion after the last period).
:h	Extract the first available pathname header (the portion before the last slash).

Modifier	Description
:t	Extract the first available pathname tail (the portion after the last slash).

Programmable Completion

Bash and the *readline* library provide *completion* facilities, whereby you can type part of a command name, hit the Tab key, and Bash fills in part or all of the rest of the command or filename. *Programmable completion* lets you, as a shell programmer, write code to customize the list of possible completions that Bash will present for a particular partially entered word. This is accomplished through the combination of several facilities:

- The **complete** command allows you to provide a completion specification, or *compspec*, for individual commands. You specify, via various options, how to tailor the list of possible completions for the particular command. This is simple, but adequate for many needs. (See the entry for **complete** on page 80.)

- For more flexibility, you can use **complete -F** *funcname command*. This tells Bash to call *funcname* to provide the list of completions for *command*. You write the *funcname* function.

- Within the code for a -F function, the COMP* shell variables provide information about the current command line. COMPREPLY is an array into which the function places the final list of completion results.

- Also within the code for a -F function, you may use the **compgen** command to generate a list of results, such as "usernames that begin with **a**" or "all set variables." The intent is that such results would be used with an array assignment:

```
...
COMPREPLY=( $( compgen options arguments ) )
...
```

Compspecs may be associated with either a full pathname for a command or, more commonly, an unadorned command name (/usr/bin/man versus plain man). Completions are attempted in the following order, based on the options provided to the com- plete command:

1. If completion is attempted on an empty input line, Bash applies the compspec given with complete -E. Otherwise, it proceeds to the next step.

2. Bash first identifies the command. If a pathname is used, Bash looks to see if a compspec exists for the full path- name. Otherwise, it sets the command name to the last component of the pathname, and searches for a compspec for the command name.

3. If a compspec exists, Bash uses it. If not, Bash uses the "default" compspec given with complete -D. If there is none, then Bash falls back to the default built-in completions.

4. Bash performs the action indicated by the compspec to generate a list of possible matches. Of this list, only those that have the word being completed as a prefix are used for the list of possible completions. For the -d and -f options, Bash uses the variable FIGNORE to filter out unde- sirable matches.

5. Bash generates filenames as specified by the -G option. GLOBIGNORE is not used to filter the results, but FIGNORE is.

6. Bash processes the argument string provided to -W. The string is split using the characters in $IFS. The resulting list provides the candidates for completion. This is often used to provide a list of options that a command accepts.

7. Bash runs functions and commands as specified by the -F and -C options. For both, Bash sets COMP_LINE and COMP_POINT as described in the section "Built-In Shell Variables" on page 32. For a shell function, COMP_WORDS and COMP_CWORD are also set.

   Also, for both functions and commands, $1 is the name of the command whose arguments are being completed, $2 is the word being completed, and $3 is the word in front of the word being completed. Bash does *not* filter the results of the command or function:

   a. Functions named with -F are run first. The function should set the COMPREPLY array to the list of possible completions. Bash retrieves the list from there.

   b. Commands provided with -C are run next, in an environment equivalent to command substitution. The command should print the list of possible completions, one per line. An embedded newline should be escaped with a backslash.

8. Once the list is generated, Bash filters the results according to the -X option. The argument to -X is a pattern specifying files to exclude. By prefixing the pattern with a !, the sense is reversed, and the pattern instead specifies that only matching files should be retained in the list. The value of the nocasematch shell option is honored.

   An & in the pattern is replaced with the text of the word being completed. Use \& to produce a literal &.

9. Finally, Bash prepends or appends any prefixes or suffixes supplied with the -P or -S options.

10. In the case that no matches were generated, if -o dirnames was used, Bash attempts directory name completion.

11. On the other hand, if -o plusdirs was provided, Bash *adds* the result of directory completion to the previously generated list.

12. Normally, when a compspec is provided, Bash's default completions are not attempted, nor are the *readline* library's default filename completions. However:

    a. If the compspec produces no results and `-o bashdefault` was provided, then Bash attempts its default completions.

    b. If neither the compspec nor the Bash default completions with `-o bashdefault` produced any results, and `-o default` was provided, then Bash has the *readline* library attempt its filename completions.

A compspec may be modified with the **compopt** command. When used without command names inside an executing completion, it affects the executing completion.

When a shell function used as a completion handler returns 124, Bash retries the completion process from the beginning. This is most useful with the default completion handler (`complete -D`) to dynamically build up a set of completions instead of loading a large set at startup. The *bash*(1) manpage has an example at the end of its *Programmable Completion* section.

Tip

Ian Macdonald has collected a large set of useful compspecs, often distributed as the file */etc/bash_completion*. If your system does not have it, you may be able to install it with your system's package manager. In the worst case, you can download it from *http://bash-completion.alioth.debian.org/*. It is worth reviewing.

Examples

Restrict files for the C compiler to C, C++, and assembler source files, and relocatable object files:

```
complete -f -X '!*.[Ccos]' gcc cc
```

For the man command, restrict expansions to things that have manpages:

```
# Simple example of programmable completion for manual
# pages.  A more elaborate example appears in the
# bash_completion file.
# Assumes   man [num] command   command syntax.

shopt -s extglob       # Enable extended pattern matching

# Define completion function
_man () {
 # Local variables
 local dir mandir=/usr/share/man

 # Clear reply list
 COMPREPLY=(  )

 # If section number ...
 if [[ ${COMP_WORDS[1]} = +([0-9]) ]]
 then
     # section provided: man 3 foo
     # look in specified directory
     dir=$mandir/man${COMP_WORDS[COMP_CWORD-1]}
 else
     # no section, default to commands
     # look in command directories
     dir=$mandir/'man[18]'
 fi
 COMPREPLY=( $(
   # Generate raw file list
   find $dir -type f |

       # Remove leading directories
       sed 's;..*/;;' |

           # Remove trailing suffixes
           sed 's/\.[0-9].*$//' |

               # Keep those that match given prefix
               grep "^${COMP_WORDS[$COMP_CWORD]}" |
```

```
                # Sort final list
                sort
    ) )
}

# Associate function with command
complete -F _man man
```

Job Control

Job control lets you place foreground jobs in the background, bring background jobs to the foreground, or suspend running jobs. All modern Unix systems—including Mac OS X, GNU/ Linux and BSD systems—support it, so the job control features are automatically enabled. Many job control commands take a *jobID* as an argument, which can be specified as follows:

%*n*   Job number *n*

%*s*   Job whose command line starts with string *s*

%?*s*   Job whose command line contains string *s*

%%   Current job

%+   Current job (same as %%)

%   Current job (same as %%)

%-   Previous job

The shell provides the following job control commands (for more information on these commands, see the section "Built-In Commands" on page 70):

bg   Put the current job in the background.

fg   Put the current job in the foreground.

jobs
    List active jobs.

kill

   Terminate a job.

stty tostop

   Stop background jobs if they try to send output to the terminal emulator. (Note that stty is not a built-in command.)

suspend

   Suspend a job-control shell (such as one created by su).

wait

   Wait for background jobs to finish.

CTRL-Z

   Suspend a foreground job. Then use bg or fg. (Your terminal emulator may use something other than CTRL-Z as
   the suspend character, but this is unlikely.)

Shell Options

Bash provides a number of shell options, settings that you
can change to modify the shell's behavior. You control these
options with the shopt command (see the entry for shopt on
page 119).

The compat*NN* options are all mutually exclusive with each
other. The compatibility level indicates a minimum level. For
example, at compat40, the shell behaves like Bash 4.0 for the features affected by compatibility settings that changed after 4.0.
Use of BASH_COMPAT is preferred.

The following descriptions describe the behavior when set.
Options marked with a dagger (†) are enabled by default:

autocd

   When the first word of a simple command cannot be executed, try to cd to it. If there is a function named cd, Bash
   will run it instead of calling the built-in cd.

cdable_vars

> Treat a nondirectory argument to **cd** as a variable whose value is the directory to go to.

cdspell

> Attempt spelling correction on each directory component of an argument to **cd**. Allowed in interactive shells only.

checkhash

> Check that commands found in the hash table still exist before attempting to use them. If not, perform a normal PATH search.

checkjobs

> When an attempt is made to exit a shell and there are stopped or running background jobs, the shell prints There are running jobs. and a list of jobs and their statuses. A second exit attempt (such as typing *EOF* again) causes the shell to exit.

checkwinsize

> Check the window size after each command, and update LINES and COLUMNS if the size has changed. This works in both interactive and noninteractive shells.

cmdhist †

> Save all lines of a multiline command in one history entry. This permits easy re-editing of multiline commands.

compat31

> Restore the behavior of the =~ operator for the [[ ]] command whereby the righthand side is always treated as a regular expression to be matched. In addition, the < and > operators ignore the locale when doing string comparison.

compat32

> Cause the < and > operators of the [[ ]] command to ignore the locale when doing string comparison. In addition, interrupting a command in the middle of a command list such as cmd1; cmd2; cmd3 does not abort execution of the entire list.

compat40

> Cause the < and > operators of the [[ ]] command to ignore the locale when doing string comparison.

compat41

> In POSIX mode, treat single quotes inside a double-quoted parameter expansion as quoting characters. There must be an even number of single quotes, and their contents are treated as quoted.

compat42

> Do not process the replacement string in a pattern substitution word expansion using quote removal.

compat43

> Do not print a warning message when using a quoted compound assignment in an argument to declare; treat word expansion errors as nonfatal, causing the current command to fail, even in POSIX mode; and do not reset the loop state inside a function, causing break and continue in a function to affect loops in the function's caller.

complete_fullquote †

> When performing filename completion, quote all shell metacharacters with preceding backslashes. If disabled, dollar signs (and possibly other characters) are not quoted, so that shell variable expansion occurs as expected.

direxpand

> When performing filename completion, replace directory names with the results of word expansion, modifying the *readline* editing buffer.

dirspell

> Attempt spelling correction on directory names during word completion if the name as given does not exist.

dotglob

> Include filenames starting with a period in the results of filename expansion.

execfail

Do not exit a noninteractive shell if the command given to **exec** cannot be executed. Interactive shells do not exit in such a case, no matter the setting of this option.

expand_aliases †

Expand aliases created with **alias**. Disabled in noninteractive shells.

Enable behavior needed for debuggers:

extdebug

- **declare -F** displays the source filename and line number for each function name argument.

- When a command run by the DEBUG trap fails, the next command is skipped.

- When a command run by the DEBUG trap inside a shell function or script sourced with . (dot) or **source** returns with an exit status of 2, the shell simulates a call to **return**.

- BASH_ARGC and BASH_ARGV are set as described earlier.

- Function tracing is enabled. Command substitutions, shell functions, and subshells invoked via (...) inherit the DEBUG and RETURN traps.

- Error tracing is enabled. Command substitutions, shell functions, and subshells invoked via (...) inherit the ERR trap.

extglob

Enable extended pattern-matching facilities such as +(...). Enabled automatically in POSIX mode. (These were not in the original Bourne shell; thus Bash requires you to enable them if you want them.)

extquote †

Allow $'...' and $"..." within ${*variable*} expansions inside double quotes.

---

failglob

Cause patterns that do not match filenames to produce an error.

force_fignore †

When doing completion, ignore words matching the list of suffixes in FIGNORE, even if such words are the only possible completions.

globasciiranges

Expand ranges used in pattern matching bracket expressions as if they were in the "C" locale, ignoring the current locale's collating sequence. This will be enabled by default in Bash 5.0.

globstar

Enable extended directory and subdirectory matching with the special ** pattern.

gnu_errfmt

Print error messages in the standard GNU format. Enabled automatically when Bash runs in an Emacs terminal window.

histappend

Append the history list to the file named by $HISTFILE upon exit, instead of overwriting the file.

histreedit

Allow a user to re-edit a failed csh-style history substitution with the *readline* library.

histverify

Place the results of csh-style history substitution into the *readline* library's editing buffer instead of executing it directly, in case the user wishes to modify it further.

hostcomplete †

If using *readline*, attempt hostname completion when a word containing an @ is being completed.

huponexit

Send a SIGHUP to all running jobs upon exiting an interactive login shell.

inherit_errexit

Cause command substitution to inherit the value of set -e. Enabled automatically in POSIX mode.

interactive_comments †

Allow words beginning with # to start a comment in an interactive shell.

lastpipe

In non-job control shells, run the last command of a foreground pipeline in the current shell environment. All commands but the last run in subshells.

lithist

If cmdhist is also set, save multiline commands to the history file with newlines instead of semicolons.

login_shell

Set by the shell when it is a login shell. This is a read-only option.

mailwarn

Print the message The mail in *mailfile* has been read when a file being checked for mail has been accessed since the last time Bash checked it.

no_empty_cmd_completion

If using *readline*, do *not* search $PATH when a completion is attempted on an empty line, or a line consisting solely of whitespace.

nocaseglob

Ignore letter case when doing filename matching.

nocasematch

Ignore letter case when doing pattern matching for case and [[ ]].

nullglob

Expand patterns that do not match any files to the null string, instead of using the literal pattern as an argument.

progcomp †

Enable programmable completion.

promptvars †

Perform variable, command, and arithmetic substitution on the values of PS0, PS1, PS2, and PS4.

restricted_shell

Set by the shell when it is a restricted shell. This is a read-only option.

shift_verbose

Cause shift to print an error message when the shift count is greater than the number of positional parameters.

sourcepath †

Cause the . (dot) and source commands to search $PATH in order to find the file to read and execute.

xpg_echo

Cause echo to expand escape sequences, even without the -e or -E options.

Command Execution

When you type a command, Bash looks in the following places (in this order) until it finds a match:

1. Keywords such as if and for.

2. Aliases. In POSIX mode, you can't define an alias whose name is a shell keyword, but you can define an alias that expands to a keyword (e.g., alias aslongas=while). When not in POSIX mode, Bash does allow you to define an alias for a shell keyword.

    Normally, alias expansion is enabled only in interactive shells. POSIX mode shells always enable it.

3. POSIX shells only: Special built-ins like `break` and `continue`. The list of POSIX special built-ins is `.` (dot), `:`, `break`, `continue`, `eval`, `exec`, `exit`, `export`, `readonly`, `return`, `set`, `shift`, `times`, `trap`, and `unset`. Bash adds `source`.

   An error from a POSIX special built-in causes noninteractive shells to exit.

4. Functions. When not in POSIX mode, Bash finds functions before *all* built-in commands.

5. Nonspecial built-ins such as `cd` and `test`.

6. Scripts and executable programs, for which the shell searches in the directories listed in the PATH environment variable. NOTE: In POSIX mode, tildes in $PATH elements are not expanded. Additionally, if a command in the hash table no longer exists, Bash re-searches $PATH.

7. When a command is not found, if a function named `command_not_found_handle` exists, the shell calls it, passing the command words as the function arguments.

The distinction between "special" built-in commands and non-special ones comes from POSIX. This distinction, combined with the `command` command, makes it possible to write functions that override shell built-ins, such as `cd`. For example:

```
# Shell function; found before built-in cd
cd () {
    command cd "$@"        Use real cd to change directory
    echo now in $PWD       Other stuff we want to do
}
```

If Bash exits due to receiving SIGHUP, or if the huponexit shell option is set, Bash sends a SIGHUP to all running child jobs. Use `disown -h` to prevent Bash from sending SIGHUP to a particular job.

Coprocesses

A *coprocess* is a process that runs in parallel with the shell and with which the shell can communicate. The shell starts the process in the background, connecting its standard input and output to a two-way pipe. (The coprocess's standard error is not redirected.)

There are two syntaxes for running a coprocess:

coproc *name non-simple command*   *Start a named coprocess*

coproc *command args*   *Start an unnamed coprocess*

The shell creates an array variable named *name* to hold the file descriptors for communication with the coprocess. *name*[0] is the output of the coprocess (input to the controlling shell) and *name*[1] is the input to the coprocess (output from the shell). In addition, the variable *name*_PID holds the process-ID of the coprocess. When no *name* is supplied, the shell uses COPROC.

NOTE

There can be only one active coprocess at a time.

Example

The following example demonstrates the basic usage of the coproc keyword and the related variables:

```
# Start a named coprocess in the background
$ coproc testproc (echo 1
> read aline ; echo $aline)
[1] 5090

# Show the file descriptors
$ echo ${testproc[@]}
63 60
```

```
# Show the coprocess PID
$ echo $testproc_PID
5090

# Read the first line of coprocess output and show it
$ read out <&${testproc[0]}
$ echo $out
1

# Send coprocess some input
$ echo foo >&${testproc[1]}

# Read second output line
$ read out2 <&${testproc[0]}
[1]+ Done    coproc testproc (echo 1; read aline; echo
$aline)

# Show the second output line
$ echo $out2
foo
```

Restricted Shells

A *restricted shell* is one that disallows certain actions, such as changing directory, setting PATH, or running commands whose names contain a / character.

The original V7 Bourne shell had an undocumented restricted mode. Later versions of the Bourne shell clarified the code and documented the facility. Bash also supplies a restricted mode. (See the manual page for the details.)

Shell scripts can still be run, since in that case the restricted shell calls the unrestricted version of the shell to run the script. This includes */etc/profile*, *~/.profile*, and the other startup files.

Tip

Restricted shells are not used much in practice, as they are difficult to set up correctly.

Built-In Commands

Examples to be entered as a command line are shown with the $ prompt. Otherwise, examples should be treated as code fragments that might be included in a shell script. For convenience, the reserved words used by multiline commands are also included.

Almost all built-in commands recognize the --help option and print a usage summary in response to it.

!   **Invert the sense of the following pipeline.**

```
! pipeline
```

Negate the sense of a pipeline. Returns an exit status of 0 if the pipeline exited nonzero, and an exit status of 1 if the pipeline exited zero. Typically used in if and while statements.

Example

This code prints a message if user jane is not logged on:

```
if ! who | grep jane > /dev/null
then
    echo jane is not currently logged on
fi
```

**Introduce a comment that runs to the end of the line.**

```
# text …
```

Ignore all text that follows on the same line. # is used in shell scripts as the comment character and is not really a command.

#!shell   Invoke the named interpreter to execute the script.

#! *shell* [*option*]

Used as the first line of a script to invoke the named *shell*. Anything given on the rest of the line is passed *as a single argument* to the named *shell*. For example:

    #!/bin/sh

Tip

This feature is typically implemented by the kernel, but may not be supported on some very old systems. Some systems have a limit of around 32 characters on the maximum length of *shell*.

:   Do-nothing command, used as a syntactic placeholder.

: [*arguments*]

Null command. Returns an exit status of 0. See this Example and the ones under the entry for case on page 77. The line is still processed for side effects, such as variable and command substitutions, or I/O redirection.

Example

Check whether someone is logged in:

```
if who | grep $1 > /dev/null
then :    # Do nothing if user is found
else echo "User $1 is not logged in"
fi
```

.   **Read and execute a file within the current shell.**

. *file* [*arguments*]

Read and execute lines in *file*. *file* does not have to be executable but must reside in a directory searched by $PATH. If the
sourcepath option is disabled, Bash does not search $PATH. The
arguments are stored in the positional parameters. If *file* is not
found in $PATH, Bash looks in the current directory for *file*.
(Note that POSIX shells do not do so.) Bash removes zero
(ASCII NUL) bytes from the contents of *file* before attempting
to parse it. Noninteractive POSIX-mode shells exit if *file* is not
found, unless prefixed with command. See also the entry for
source on page 120.

When the -T option is set, traps on DEBUG are inherited, and any
changes made to the DEBUG trap by *file* remain in place upon
return to the calling shell. If -T is not set, DEBUG traps are saved
and restored around the call to *file*, and DEBUG trap is unset
while *file* executes.

[[ ]]   **Extended version of the test command.**

[[*expression*]]

Same as test *expression* or [*expression*], except that [[ ]]
allows additional operators. Word splitting and filename
expansion are disabled. Note that the brackets ([ ]) are typed
literally, and that they must be surrounded by whitespace. See
the entry for test on page 120.

Additional Operators

&&   Logical AND of test expressions (short circuit).

|| Logical OR of test expressions (short circuit).

<   First string is lexically "less than" the second, based on the locale's sorting order. (However, see the description of the compat31, compat32, and compat40 options in the section "Shell Options" on page 60.)

>   First string is lexically "greater than" the second, based on the locale's sorting order. (However, see the description of the compat31, compat32, and compat40 options in the section "Shell Options" on page 60.)

---

name ( )   Define a shell function.

```
name () { commands; } [redirections]
```

Define *name* as a function. POSIX syntax. The function definition can be written on one line or across many. You may also provide the function keyword, an alternate form that works similarly. See the section "Functions" on page 23.

Example

```
$ countfiles () {
>     ls | wc -l
> }
```

When issued at the command line, countfiles displays the number of files in the current directory.

alias

Define and manage shell aliases.

```
alias [-p] [name[='cmd']]
```

Assign a shorthand *name* as a synonym for *cmd*. If =`'cmd'` is
omitted, print the alias for *name*; if *name* is also omitted, print
all aliases. If the alias value contains a trailing space, the next
word on the command line also becomes a candidate for alias
expansion. The BASH_ALIASES array provides programmatic
access to all defined aliases; see the section "Built-In Shell Variables" on page 32. See also the entry for unalias on page 130.

Tip

In general, functions are preferred to aliases; they let you have
local variables and are fully programmable.

Option

-p   Print the word alias before each alias.

Example

```
alias dir='echo ${PWD##*/}'
```

---

bg

Move a stopped job into the background.

```
bg [jobIDs]
```

Put current job or *jobIDs* in the background. See the section
"Job Control" on page 59.

```
bind [-m map] [options]
bind [-m map] [-q function] [-r sequence]
              [-u function]
bind [-m map] -f file
bind [-m map] -x sequence:command
bind [-m map] sequence:function
bind readline-command
```

Manage the *readline* library. Nonoption arguments have the same form as in a *.inputrc* file.

Options

-f *file*

  Read key bindings from *file*.

-l List the names of all the *readline* functions.

-m *map*

  Use *map* as the keymap. Available keymaps are emacs, emacs-ctlx, emacs-standard, emacs-meta, vi, vi-command, vi-insert, and vi-move. vi is the same as vi-command, and emacs is the same as emacs-standard.

-p Print the current *readline* bindings such that they can be reread from a *.inputrc* file.

-P Print the current *readline* bindings.

-q *function*

  Query which keys invoke the *readline* function *function*.

-r *sequence*

  Remove the binding for key sequence *sequence*.

-s Print the current *readline* key sequence and macro bindings such that they can be reread from a *.inputrc* file.

-S Print the current *readline* key sequence and macro bindings.

-u *function*
　　Unbind all keys that invoke the *readline* function *function*.

-v　　Print the current *readline* variables such that they can be reread from a *.inputrc* file.

-V　　Print the current *readline* variables.

-x *sequence:command*
　　Execute the shell command *command* whenever *sequence* is entered. The *command* may make use of and modify the READLINE_LINE and READLINE_POINT variables. Changes to these variables are reflected in the editing state.

-X　　Print the current *readline* key sequences bound with -x such that they can be reread from a *.inputrc* file.

---

break   Exit from one or more loops.

```
break [n]
```

Exit from a for, while, select, or until loop (or break out of *n* nested loops).

---

builtin   Execute a built-in command, bypassing functions.

```
builtin command [arguments ...]
```

Run the shell built-in command *command* with the given arguments. This allows you to bypass any functions that redefine a built-in command's name. The command command is more portable.

Example

This function lets you do your own tasks when you change directory:

```
cd () {
    builtin cd "$@"        # Actually change directory
    pwd                    # Report location
}
```

---

caller   Print function or dot-file caller, for use with the Bash debugger.

    caller [expression]

Print the line number and source filename of the current function call or dot file. With nonzero *expression*, print that element
from the call stack. The most recent is zero. This command is
for use by the Bash debugger.

---

case   Syntax for a case statement.

    case value in
    [(]pattern1) cmds1;;   # ;& or ;;& -- see text
    [(]pattern2) cmds2;;
        . . .
    esac

Execute the first set of commands (*cmds1*) if *value* matches *pat-
tern1*; execute the second set of commands (*cmds2*) if *value*
matches *pattern2*, and so on. Be sure the last command in each
set ends with ;;. *value* is typically a positional parameter or
other shell variable. *cmds* are typically executable commands,
shell programming commands, or variable assignments. Patterns can use file-generation metacharacters. Multiple patterns
(separated by |) can be specified on the same line; in this case,
the associated *cmds* are executed whenever *value* matches any
of these patterns. See the Examples here and under the entry
for eval on page 90.

The shell allows *pattern* to be preceded by an optional open
parenthesis, as in (*pattern*). For some shell versions, it's necessary for balancing parentheses inside a $( ) construct. Bash 4.0

and later do not require it. See also the `nocasematch` option in the section "Shell Options" on page 60.

Bash provides two additional special terminators for the *cmds* in a `case` statement: `;&` causes execution to continue into the next set of *cmds*, and `;;&` causes the next *pattern* list to be tested.

Examples

Check first command-line argument and take appropriate action:

```
case $1 in      # Match the first arg
no|yes)  response=1;;
-[tT])   table=TRUE;;
*)       echo "unknown option"; exit 1;;
esac
```

Read user-supplied lines until user exits:

```
while true
do      printf "Type . to finish ==> "
        read line
        case "$line" in
        .) echo "Message done"
           break ;;
        *) echo "$line" >> $message ;;
        esac
done
```

---

cd   **Change directory.**

```
cd [-L] [-P [-e]] [-@] [dir]
cd [-L] [-P [-e]] [-@] [-]
```

With no arguments, change to home directory of user. Otherwise, change working directory to *dir*. Bash searches the directories given in $CDPATH first, and then looks in the current directory for *dir*. If *dir* is a relative pathname but is not in the

---

current directory, then also search $CDPATH. A directory of -
stands for the previous directory. This command exits with a
failure status if PWD is read-only.

Options

-e   With -P, if the current directory cannot be determined,
     exit with a failure value.

-L   Use the logical path (what the user typed, including any
     symbolic links) for cd .. and the value of PWD. This is the
     default.

-P   Use the filesystem physical path for cd .. and the value of
     PWD.

-@   On systems supporting extended attributes, treat a file
     with extended attributes as a directory containing the file's
     attributes.

Example

```
$ ls -ld /var/run                          /var/run is a symbolic link
lrwxrwxrwx 1 root root 4 May  7 19:41 /var/run -> /run
$ cd -L /var/run                           Logical change directory
$ pwd                                      Show location
/var/run                                   Result is logical location
$ cd -P /var/run                           Physical change directory
$ pwd                                      Show location
/run                                       Result is physical location
```

---

command   Execute or print information about a built-in command.

    command [-pvV] name [arg ...]

Without -v or -V, execute *name* with given arguments. This
command bypasses any aliases or functions that may be
defined for *name*. When used with a special built-in, it prevents
the built-in from exiting the script if it fails. In POSIX mode,

assignments given as arguments to the `alias`, `declare`, `export`, `local`, `readonly`, and `typeset` commands still take effect, even when preceded by `command`.

Options

-p   Use a predefined default search path, not the current value of PATH.

-v   Print a description of how the shell interprets *name*.

-V   Print a more verbose description of how the shell interprets *name*.

Example

Create an alias for `rm` that gets the system's version, and run it with the `-i` option:

```
$ alias 'rm=command -p rm -i'
```

---

compgen   Generate possible completions.

```
compgen [options] [string]
```

Generate possible completions for *string* according to the options. Options are those accepted by `complete`, except for -p and -r. For more information, see the entry for `complete` on page 80.

---

complete   Specify how to do completion for specific commands.

```
complete [-DE] [options] command …
```

Specify how to complete arguments for each *command*. This is discussed in the section "Programmable Completion" on page 54.

Options

-a   Same as -A alias.

-A *type*

     Use *type* to specify a list of possible completions. The *type* may be one of the following:

alias	Alias names
arrayvar	Array variable names
binding	Bindings from the *readline* library
builtin	Shell built-in command names
command	Command names
directory	Directory names
disabled	Names of disabled shell built-in commands
enabled	Names of enabled shell built-in commands
export	Exported variables
file	Filenames
function	Names of shell functions
group	Group names
helptopic	Help topics as allowed by the help built-in command
hostname	Hostnames, as found in the file named by $HOSTFILE
job	Job names
keyword	Shell reserved keywords
running	Names of running jobs
service	Service names (from */etc/services*)
setopt	Valid arguments for set -o
shopt	Valid option names for the shopt built-in command
signal	Signal names
stopped	Names of stopped jobs

user	Usernames
variable	Shell variable names

-b   Same as -A builtin.

-c   Same as -A command.

-C *command*

     Run *command* in a subshell and use its output as the list of completions.

-d   Same as -A directory.

-D   Apply the rest of the options and parameters to the "default" completion, which is used when no other comp-spec can be found.

-e   Same as -A export.

-E   Apply the rest of the options and parameters to the "empty" completion, which is used when completion is attempted on an empty input line.

-f   Same as -A file.

-F *function*

     Run shell function *function* in the current shell. Upon its return, retrieve the list of completions from the COMPREPLY array.

-g   Same as -A group.

-G *pattern*

     Expand *pattern* to generate completions.

-j   Same as -A job.

-k   Same as -A keyword.

-o *option*

     Control the behavior of the completion specification. The value for *option* is one of the following:

bashdefault	Fall back to the normal Bash completions if no matches are produced.
default	Use the default *readline* completions if no matches are produced.
dirnames	Do directory name completion if no matches are produced.
filenames	Inform the *readline* library that the intended output is filenames, so the library can do any filename-specific processing, such as adding a trailing slash for directories or removing trailing spaces.
noquote	Inform the *readline* library that it should not quote completed words that are filenames.
nosort	Inform the *readline* library that it should not sort the list of completed words.
nospace	Inform the *readline* library that it should not append a space to words completed at the end of a line.
plusdirs	Attempt directory completion and add any results to the list of completions already generated.

-p   With no commands, print all completion settings in a way that can be reread.

-P *prefix*

Prepend *prefix* to each resulting string after all the other options have been applied.

-r   Remove the completion settings for the given commands, or all settings if no commands.

-s   Same as -A service.

-S *suffix*

Append *suffix* to each resulting string after all the other options have been applied.

-u   Same as -A user.

-v   Same as -A variable.

-W *wordlist*

> Split *wordlist* (a single shell word) using $IFS. The generated list contains the members of the split list that matched the word being completed. Each member is then expanded using brace expansion, tilde expansion, parameter and variable expansion, command substitution, and arithmetic expansion. Shell quoting is respected.

-X *pattern*

> Exclude filenames matching *pattern* from the filename completion list. With a leading !, the sense is reversed, and only filenames matching *pattern* are retained.

Tip

Courtesy of Chet Ramey. Use:

```
complete -A helptopic help
```

to restrict the set of possible completions for the help command to the set of help topics. Upon doing so, typing help and two Tabs causes the shell to display the list of help topics.

---

compopt **Print or change the completion options for a command.**

```
compopt [-DE] [-o options] [+o options]
        [commands …]
```

With no options, print the completion options for one or more *commands*, or for the currently executing completion when invoked without *commands*. With options, modify the existing compspecs for the given *commands*, or for the currently executing completion when invoked without *commands*.

Options

-D Apply the *options* to the "default" completion.

-E Apply the *options* to the "empty" completion.

-o *option*

> Enable *option*, which is one of the valid options for the `complete` command.

+o *option*

> Disable *option*, which is one of the valid options for the `complete` command.

---

continue   Skip the rest of the body of one or more loops.

```
continue [n]
```

Skip remaining commands in a `for`, `while`, `select`, or `until` loop, resuming with the next iteration of the loop (or skipping *n* nested loops).

---

declare   Declare shell variables and manage their attributes.

```
declare [options] [name[=value]]
```

Declare variables and manage their attributes. In function bodies, variables are local, as if declared with the `local` command. All options must be given first. See also the entry for `typeset` on page 128.

Options

-a   Each *name* is an indexed array.

-A   Each *name* is an associative array.

-f   Each *name* is a function.

-F   For functions, print just the function's name and attributes, not the function definition (body).

-g   When used inside a function, declare the variable in the global scope, instead of at the local scope.

-i   Each variable is an integer; in an assignment, the value is
      evaluated as an arithmetic expression.

-l   Mark *names* to have their values converted to lowercase
      upon assignment.

-n   Each *name* is a nameref. See the section "Indirect Vari-
      ables (namerefs)" on page 31.

-p   With no *names*, print all variables, their values, and
      attributes. With *names*, print the names, attributes, and
      values (if set) of the given variables. With -f, print func-
      tion definitions.

-r   Mark *names* as read-only. Subsequent assignments will
      fail, and read-only variables cannot be unset.

-t   Apply the *trace* attribute to each name. Traced functions
      inherit the DEBUG trap. This attribute has no meaning for
      variables.

-u   Mark *names* to have their values converted to uppercase
      upon assignment.

-x   Mark *names* for export into the environment of child
      processes.

With a + instead of a -, the given attribute is disabled.

With no variable names, all variables having the given
attribute(s) are printed in a form that can be reread as input to
the shell.

Examples

```
$ declare -i val                    Make val an integer
$ val=4+7                           Evaluate value
$ echo $val                         Show result
11

$ declare -r z=42                   Make z read-only
$ z=31                              Try to assign to it
bash: z: readonly variable          Assignment fails
```

```
$ echo $z
42

$ declare -p val z                    Show attributes and values
declare -i val="11"
declare -r z="42"
```

---

dirs   Print or manage the directory stack.

    dirs [-clpv] [+n] [-n]

Print the directory stack, which is managed with pushd and
popd.

Options

+n   Print the nth entry from the left; first entry is zero.

-n   Print the nth entry from the right; first entry is zero.

-c   Clear (remove all entries from) the directory stack.

-l   Produce a longer listing, one that does not replace $HOME
      with ~.

-p   Print the directory stack, one entry per line.

-v   Print the directory stack, one entry per line, with each
      entry preceded by its index in the stack.

---

disown   Stop managing one or more jobs.

    disown [-ahr] [job …]

Remove one or more *jobs* from the list of jobs managed by
Bash. A *job* is either a job specification or a process-ID.

Options

-a   Remove all jobs. With -h, mark all jobs.

-h   Instead of removing jobs from the list of known jobs, mark them to *not* receive SIGHUP as described in the section "Command Execution" on page 66.

-r   With no jobs, remove (or mark) only running jobs.

---

do   **Reserved word that starts the body of a loop.**

    do

Reserved word that precedes the command sequence in a for, while, until, or select statement.

---

done   **Reserved word that ends the body of a loop.**

    done

Reserved word that ends a for, while, until, or select statement.

---

echo   **Print command-line arguments to standard output.**

    echo [-eEn] [*string*]

Write *string* to standard output. This is the built-in version of the command. (It is likely that you also have a standalone executable program named echo for which you should see your local *echo*(1) man page.)

Options

If the xpg_echo shell option is set, along with POSIX mode (set -o posix), echo does not interpret any options.

-e Enable interpretation of the escape sequences as described in the section "Escape Sequences" on page 12. They must be quoted (or escaped with a \) to prevent interpretation by the shell.

-E Do not interpret escape sequences, even on systems where the default behavior of the built-in echo is to interpret them.

-n Do not print the terminating newline.

Examples

```
$ echo "testing printer" | lpr
$ echo -e "Warning: ringing bell \a"
```

---

enable   Enable or disable shell built-in commands.

    enable [-adnps] [-f file] [command ...]

Enable or disable shell built-in commands. Disabling a built-in lets you use an external version of a command that would otherwise use a built-in version, such as echo or test.

Options

-a For use with -p; print information about all built-in commands, disabled and enabled.

-d Remove (delete) a built-in previously loaded with -f.

-f file
    Load a new built-in command *command* from the shared library file *file*. The shell searches for *file* in the directories named in $BASH_LOADABLES_PATH.

-n Disable the named built-in commands.

-p   Print a list of enabled built-in commands.

-s   Print only the POSIX special built-in commands. When combined with -f, the new built-in command becomes a POSIX special built-in.

---

esac   Reserved word that ends a case statement.

```
esac
```

Reserved word that ends a case statement.

---

eval   Rescan and execute an already-processed input line.

```
eval args
```

Typically, eval is used in shell scripts, and *args* is a line of code that contains shell variables. eval forces variable expansion to happen first and then runs the resulting command. This "double-scanning" is useful any time shell variables contain input/output redirection symbols, aliases, or other shell variables. (For example, redirection normally happens before variable expansion, so a variable containing redirection symbols must be expanded first using eval; otherwise, the redirection symbols remain uninterpreted.)

Example

This fragment of a shell script shows how eval constructs a command that is interpreted in the correct order:

```
for option
do
    # Define where output goes
    case "$option" in
    save) out=' > $newfile' ;;
    show) out=' | more' ;;
    esac
done

eval sort $file $out
```

---

exec   Replace the current script or manage shell file descriptors.

```
exec [command args …]
exec [-a name] [-cl] [command args … ]
exec redirections …
```

Execute *command* in place of the current process (instead of creating a new process). With only redirections (see the section "Redirection using file descriptors" on page 19), **exec** is also useful for opening, closing, copying, or moving file descriptors. In this case, the script continues to run.

Options

-a   Use *name* for the value of *command*'s argv[0].

-c   Clear the environment before executing the program.

-l   Place a minus sign at the front of *command*'s argv[0], just as *login*(1) does.

Examples

trap 'exec 2>&-' 0   *Close stderr when script exits (signal 0)*

$ **exec /bin/csh**   *Replace shell with C shell (bad idea)*
$ **exec < infile**   *Reassign standard input to infile*

exit
Exit the shell script.

```
exit [n]
```

Exit a shell script with status *n* (e.g., exit 1). *n* can be 0 (success) or nonzero (failure). If *n* is not given, the shell's exit status is that of the most recent command. exit can be issued at the command line to close a window (log out). Exit statuses can range in value from 0 to 255. Any trap on EXIT executes before the shell exits. Noninteractive login shells execute *~/.bash_logout* if it exists. See also the section "Command Exit Status" on page 6.

Example

```
if [ $# -eq 0 ]
then
    echo "Usage: $0 [-c] [-d] file(s)" 1>&2
    exit 1                  # Error status
fi
```

export
Export items or print information about exported items.

```
export [variables]
export [name=[value] ...]
export -p
export [-fn] [name=[value] ...]
```

Pass (export) the value of one or more shell *variables*, giving global meaning to the variables (which are local by default). For example, a variable defined in one shell script must be exported if its value is used in other programs called by the script. If no *variables* are given, export lists the variables exported by the current shell. The second form is the POSIX version, which is similar to the first form, except that you can set a variable *name* to a *value* before exporting it. export can also export functions.

Options

-f   Names refer to functions; the functions are exported into the environment.

-n   Remove the named variables or functions from the environment.

-p   Print declare -x before printing the names and values of exported variables. This allows saving a list of exported variables for rereading later. Print only the names of exported functions, not their bodies.

Examples

In the original Bourne shell, you would type:

```
TERM=vt100
export TERM
```

In Bash, you type this instead:

```
export TERM=vt100
```

---

false   Exit with a false (failure) return value.

```
false
```

Built-in command that exits with a false return value.

---

fc   Manage command-line history.

```
fc [options] [first [last]]
fc -e - [old=new] [command]
fc -s [old=new] [command]
```

Display or edit commands in the history list. (Use only one of -e, -l, or -s.)

first and *last* are numbers or strings specifying the range of commands to display or edit. If *last* is omitted, fc applies to a single command (specified by *first*). If both *first* and *last* are omitted, fc edits the previous command or lists the last 16. If *first* is -0, it relates to the current command.

The second form of fc takes a history *command*, replaces *old* with *new*, and executes the modified command. If no strings are specified, *command* is just re-executed. If no *command* is given either, the previous command is re-executed. *command* is a number or string like *first*. See the Examples in the section "Command History" on page 49. The third form is equivalent to the second form.

Options

-e *editor*

Invoke *editor* to edit the specified history commands. You must supply an editor name with -e. Without -e, fc invokes the default editor, which is set by the shell variable FCEDIT. If that variable is not set, Bash tries $EDITOR. If neither is set, the default editor is vi. Versions 3.1 and newer default to ed when in POSIX mode.

-e -

Execute (or redo) a history command; refer to the second syntax line above.

-l   List the specified command or range of commands, or list the last 16.

-n   Suppress command numbering from the -l listing.

-r   Reverse the order of the -l listing.

-s   Equivalent to -e -.

fg   Move a running or suspended background job into the foreground.

```
fg [jobIDs]
```

Bring current job or *jobIDs* to the foreground. See the section "Job Control" on page 59.

---

fi   Reserved word that ends an if statement.

```
fi
```

Reserved word that ends an if statement.

---

for   Start a loop over a list of values.

```
for x [in [list]]
do
    commands
done
```

For variable *x* (in optional *list* of values), do *commands*. If in *list* is omitted, "$@" (the positional parameters) is assumed. If the expansion of *list* is empty, no *commands* execute.

Examples

Paginate files specified on the command line, and save each result:

```
for file
do
    pr $file > $file.tmp
done
```

Same, but put entire loop into the background:

```
for file
do
    pr $file > $file.tmp
done &
```

Search chapters for a list of words (like fgrep -f):

```
for item in $(cat program_list)
do
    echo "Checking chapters for"
    echo "references to program $item…"
    grep -c "$item.[co]" chap*
done
```

Extract a one-word title from each file named on the command line and use it as the new filename:

```
for file
do
    name=$(sed -n 's/NAME: //p' $file)
    mv $file $name
done
```

---

for   **Start an arithmetic loop.**

```
for ((init; cond; incr))
do
    commands
done
```

Arithmetic for loop, similar to C's. Evaluate *init*. While *cond* is true, execute the body of the loop. Evaluate *incr* before retesting *cond*. Any one of the expressions may be omitted; a missing *cond* is treated as being true.

Example

Search for a phrase in each odd chapter:

```
for ((x=1; x <= 20; x += 2))
do
    grep $1 chap$x
done
```

---

function   Define a shell function.

```
function name { commands; } [redirections]
function name () { commands; } [redirections]
```

Define *name* as a shell function. See the description of function
semantics in the section "Functions" on page 23.

Example

Define a function to count files.

```
$ function countfiles {
>     ls | wc -l
> }
```

---

getopts   Process command-line options and arguments.

```
getopts string name [args]
```

Process command-line arguments (or *args*, if specified) and
check for legal options. getopts is used in shell script loops
and is intended to ensure standard syntax for command-line
options.

Standard syntax dictates that command-line options begin with
a -. Options can be stacked (i.e., consecutive letters can follow a
single -). You end processing of options by specifying -- on the
command line. *string* contains the option letters to be recog-
nized by getopts when running the shell script. Valid options
are processed in turn and stored in the shell variable *name*. If
name is read-only, the command exits with a return value of 2.

If an option character in the options string is followed by a colon, the actual option must be followed by one or more arguments. (Multiple arguments must be given to the command as one shell *word*. This is done by quoting the arguments or separating them with commas. The script must be written to expect multiple arguments in this format.)

getopts uses the shell variables OPTARG, OPTIND, and OPTERR (see the section "Built-In Shell Variables" on page 32).

---

hash   Manage the table of previously found commands.

```
hash [-dlrt] [commands]
hash [-p file] [command]
```

As the shell finds commands along the search path ($PATH), it remembers the found locations in an internal hash table. The next time you enter a command, the shell uses the value stored in its hash table.

With no arguments, hash lists the current set of hashed commands. The display shows *hits* (the number of times the command has been called by the shell) and the command name. If the table is empty, then if Bash is in POSIX mode, hash prints nothing. Otherwise, it prints hash: hash table empty on standard output.

With *commands*, the shell adds those commands to the hash table. With no options and just *commands*, the shell resets the "hit count" associated with each command to zero.

The BASH_CMDS array provides programmatic access to all entries in the hash table; see the section "Built-In Shell Variables" on page 32.

Options

-d   Delete (remove) just the specified commands from the hash table.

-l   Produce output in a format that can be reread to rebuild the hash table.

-p *file*
    Associate *file* with *command* in the hash table.

-r   Remove all commands from the hash table.

-t   With one name, print the full pathname of the command. With more than one name, print the name and the full path, in two columns.

Tip

Besides the -r option, the hash table is also cleared when PATH is assigned. Use PATH=$PATH to clear the hash table without affecting your search path. This is most useful if you have installed a new version of a command in a directory that is earlier in $PATH than the current version of the command.

---

help   Print command usage information.

    help [-dms] [*pattern*]

Print usage information on standard output for each command that matches *pattern*. The information includes descriptions of each command's options.

Options

-d   Print a brief description of what the command does.

-m   Print the full description of the command in a format similar to that of a Unix manual page.

-s   Print short (brief) usage information.

Examples

```
$ help -s cd                    Short help
cd: cd [-L|[-P [-e]] [-@]] [dir]

$ help true                     Full help
true: true
    Return a successful result.

    Exit Status:
    Always succeeds.
```

---

history   Print command-line history.

```
history [count]
history [options]
```

Print commands in the history list or manage the history file. With no options or arguments, display the history list with command numbers. With a *count* argument, print only that many of the most recent commands.

Bash stores the command history for any shell where history is enabled (with set -o history) and HISTFILE is set, not just interactive shells.

Options

-a   Append new history lines (those executed since the history file was last written) to the history file. The write happens immediately.

-c   Clear the history list (remove all entries).

-d *position*
      Delete the history item at position *position*.

-n   Read unread history lines from the history file and append them to the history list.

-p *argument* ...

Perform csh-style history expansion on each *argument*, printing the results to standard output. The results are not saved in the history list.

-r   Read the history file and replace the history list with its contents.

-s *argument* ...

Store the *arguments* in the history list, as a single entry.

-w   Write the current history list to the history file, overwriting it entirely. The write happens immediately.

Tip

Courtesy of Eli Zaretskii. You can use

```
export PROMPT_COMMAND='history -a'
```

to ensure that the history file is always up to date, even if the user did not log out gracefully and even if the session is still alive.

---

if   **Syntax for an if-then-else statement.**

```
if condition1
then commands1
[ elif condition2
  then commands2 ]
    .
    .
    .
[ else commands3 ]
fi
```

If *condition1* is met, do *commands1*; otherwise, if *condition2* is met, do *commands2*; if neither is met, do *commands3*. Conditions are often specified with the test and [[ ]] commands. See the entries for test on page 120, and [[ ]] on page 72, for

---

a full list of conditions, and see additional Examples under the entries for : on page 71, and exit on page 92.

Examples

Insert a 0 before numbers less than 10:

```
if [ $counter -lt 10 ]
then number=0$counter
else number=$counter
fi
```

Make a directory if it doesn't exist:

```
if ! [ -d $dir ]
then
    mkdir -m 775 $dir
fi
```

---

jobs   List running or stopped jobs.

```
jobs [options] [jobIDs]
```

List all running or stopped jobs, or list those specified by *jobIDs*. For example, you can check whether a long compilation or text formatting job is still running. Also useful before logging out. See the section "Job Control" on page 59.

Options

-l   List job IDs and process group IDs.

-n   List only jobs whose status changed since last notification.

-p   List process group IDs only.

-r   List running jobs only.

-s   List stopped jobs only.

-x *cmd*

> Replace each job ID found in *cmd* with the associated process ID and then execute *cmd*.

---

kill   Send a signal to one or more jobs.

    kill [*options*] *IDs*

Terminate each specified process *ID* or job *ID*. You must own the process or be a privileged user. This built-in is similar to the external kill command, but also allows symbolic job names. Stubborn processes can (usually) be killed using signal 9. See the section "Job Control" on page 59.

The command kill -l prints a list of the available signal names. The list varies by system architecture.

The signals and their numbers are defined in the C <signal.h> header file. This file may include others, thus the actual location of the signal definitions varies across systems.

Options

-l [*n*]

> With no *n*, list the signal names. A numeric value *n* is interpreted as either a signal number, or as an exit status for a process terminated by a signal (128 + *n*). In both cases, kill prints the corresponding signal name.

-L [*n*]

> Same as -l.

-n *num*

> Send the given signal number.

-s *name*

> Send the given signal name.

-signal
> Send the given signal number (from `<signal.h>`) or signal name (from `kill -l`). With a signal number of 9, the kill is absolute.

In POSIX mode, you must leave off the SIG prefix for signal names, and `kill -l` prints all the signal names on a single line.

---

let
Perform arithmetic.

```
let expressions
(( expressions ))
```

Perform arithmetic as specified by one or more *expressions*. *expressions* consist of numbers, operators, and shell variables (which don't need a preceding $). Expressions must be quoted if they contain spaces or other special characters. The ((...)) form does the quoting for you. For more information and examples, see the section "Arithmetic Expressions" on page 47. See also *expr*(1). If the final expression evaluates to zero, `let` returns 1 (failure); otherwise it returns zero (success).

Examples

Each of these examples adds 1 to variable i:

```
i=`expr $i + 1`          All Bourne shells
let i=i+1                Bash
let "i = i + 1"
(( i = i + 1 ))
(( i += 1 ))
(( i++ ))
if (( i % 2 == 0 )) …
```

---

local
Declare local variables inside shell functions.

    local [options] [name[=value]]

Declare local variables for use inside functions. The *options* are the same as those accepted by `declare`; see the entry for `declare` on page 85 for the full list. It is an error to use `local` outside a function body.

If *name* is -, the shell saves the values of the single letter options and restores them upon function exit.

logout
Exit the shell.

    logout

Exit a login shell. Execute ~/.*bash_logout* if it exists. The command fails if the current shell is not a login shell.

mapfile
Read a file into a shell array.

    mapfile [options] [array]

Read standard input into *array*, one line per element. If no *array*, use MAPFILE. An alternate file descriptor may be given with the -u option.

Options

-c *count*

Specifies the "quantum" for the -C option. The default value is 5,000.

-C *command*

Every "quantum" lines, evaluate *command*, passing it the index in *array* that is about to be assigned, and the line that is to be assigned. The quantum is set with the -c option. (This option is mainly used by the Bash debugger.)

-d *delim*

Use *delim*'s first character to terminate input lines instead of newline. If *delim* is the null string, use the zero byte (ASCII NUL) as the delimiter.

-n *count*

Read at most *count* lines. If *count* is zero, read all the lines.

-O *index*

Fill *array* starting at origin *index*. The default origin is zero.

-s *count*

Skip (ignore) the first *count* lines.

-t Remove the trailing delimiter (usually a newline) from each line read.

-u *n*

Read from file descriptor *n* instead of from standard input.

---

popd   Pop a directory off of the directory stack.

popd [-n] [+count] [-count]

Pop the top directory off the directory stack (as shown by the dirs command), and change to the new top directory, or manage the directory stack.

Options

+*count*

Remove the item *count* entries from the left, as shown by dirs. Counting starts at zero. No directory change occurs.

-count

> Remove the item *count* entries from the right, as shown by
> dirs. Counting starts at zero. No directory change occurs.

-n   Don't change to the new top directory; just manipulate the
     stack.

---

printf   Do formatted printing of command-line arguments.

```
printf [-v var] format [val …]
```

Formatted printing, like the ANSI C printf() function (see
printf(3)). Escape sequences in *format* are expanded as
described in the section "Escape Sequences" on page 12. The
format string is reused from the beginning if there are more
values than format specifiers.

Option

-v *var*

> Save the result in *var* instead of printing it to standard out-
> put, even if the result is empty. *var* may be an array
> element.

Additional Format Letters

Bash accepts these additional format letters:

%b   Expand escape sequences in argument strings. The set of
     escape sequences is those accepted by echo -e. (See the
     section "Escape Sequences" on page 12.)

%q   Print a quoted string that can be reread later on.

%(*datefmt*)T

> Print time values using *datefmt* as the format control
> string for *strftime*(3). Use the current time if no argument
> is supplied.

pushd   Push a directory onto the directory stack.

```
pushd [-n] [directory]
pushd [-n] [+count] [-count]
```

Add *directory* to the directory stack, or rotate the directory stack. With no arguments, swap the top two entries on the stack, and change to the new top entry.

Options

+*count*

> Rotate the stack so that the *count*'th item from the left, as shown by dirs, is the new top of the stack. Counting starts at zero. The new top becomes the current directory.

-*count*

> Rotate the stack so that the *count*'th item from the right, as shown by dirs, is the new top of the stack. Counting starts at zero. The new top becomes the current directory.

-n Don't change to the new top directory; just manipulate the stack.

---

pwd   Print working directory.

```
pwd [-LP]
```

Print the current working directory on standard output. Exit with a failure status if PWD is read-only.

Options

Options give control over the use of logical versus physical treatment of the printed path. See also the entry for cd on page 78.

- -L Use the logical path (what the user typed, including any
     symbolic links) and the value of PWD for the current direc-
     tory. This is the default.

- -P Use the filesystem physical path for the current directory.

---

read   Read data into one or more shell variables.

    read [options] [variable1 [variable2 …]]

Read one line of standard input and assign each word to the
corresponding *variable*, with all leftover words assigned to the
last variable. If only one variable is specified, the entire line is
assigned to that variable. Bash removes zero (ASCII NUL)
bytes from the input. See the Examples here and under the
entry for case on page 77. The return status is 0 unless *EOF* is
reached. If no variables are given, input is stored in the REPLY
variable. In a POSIX mode shell, trapped signals can interrupt
read, in which case it returns 128 + the signal number and dis-
cards partially read input.

Options

-a *array*

> Read into indexed array *array*. Report an error if *array* is a
> preexisting associative array.

-d *delim*

> Read up to the first occurrence of *delim*, instead of new-
> line. If *delim* is the null string, use the zero byte (ASCII
> NUL) as the delimiter.

-e Use the *readline* library if reading from a terminal.

-i *text*

> When using the *readline* library, put *text* into the initial
> editing buffer.

-n *count*

Read at most *count* bytes. If a delimiter character is seen before reading *count* bytes, stop reading further input.

-N *count*

Read at most *count* bytes. Delimiter characters in the data do not cause Bash to stop reading; instead they are included in the data that is read.

-p *prompt*

Print *prompt* before reading input.

-r   Raw mode; ignore \ as a line-continuation character.

-s   Read silently; characters are not echoed.

-t *timeout*

When reading from a terminal or pipe, if no data is entered after *timeout* seconds, return 1. This prevents an application from hanging forever, waiting for user input. Values for *timeout* may be fractional. If *timeout* is zero but data is available to be read, read returns successfully. Partial input read when the *timeout* expires is saved in *variable1*; the other variables are cleared. read returns greater than 128 if no data were read and the *timeout* expires.

-u [*n*]

Read input from file descriptor *n* (default is 0).

Examples

Read three variables:

```
$ read first last address
Sarah Caldwell 123 Main Street

$ echo -e "$last, $first\n$address"
Caldwell, Sarah
123 Main Street
```

Prompt yourself to enter two temperatures:

```
$ read -p "High low: " n1 n2
High low: 65 33
```

readarray   Read a file into a shell array.

```
readarray [options] [array]
```

Identical to the mapfile command. See the entry for mapfile on page 105 for more information.

readonly   Mark variables as read only.

```
readonly [-aAfp] [variable[=value] …]
```

Prevent the specified shell variables from being assigned new values. An initial value may be supplied using the assignment syntax, but that value may not be changed subsequently. Read-only variables may not be unset.

Options

-a   Each *variable* must refer to an indexed array.

-A   Each *variable* must refer to an associative array.

-f   Each *variable* must refer to a function.

-p   Print readonly before printing the names and values of read-only variables. This allows saving a list of read-only variables for rereading later.

return   **Return an exit status from a shell function.**

```
return [n]
```

Use inside a function definition. Exit the function with status *n* or with the exit status of the previously executed command. If *n* is negative, precede it with - -.

select   **Present a menu of items for use in executing a block of code.**

```
select x [in list]
do
      commands
done
```

Display a list of menu items on standard error, numbered in the order they are specified in *list*. If no in *list* is given, items are taken from the command line (via "$@"). Following the menu is a prompt string (the value of PS3). At the $PS3 prompt, users select a menu item by typing its number, or they redisplay the menu by pressing the Enter key. User input is stored in the shell variable REPLY. If a valid item number is typed, the shell sets *x* to the chosen value and executes *commands*. Typing *EOF* terminates the loop.

Example

```
PS3="Select the item number: "
select event in Format Page View Exit
do
     case "$event" in
     Format) nroff $file | lpr;;
     Page)   pr $file | lpr;;
     View)   more $file;;
     Exit)   exit 0;;
     *  )    echo "Invalid selection";;
     esac
done
```

The output of this script looks like this:

```
1. Format
2. Page
3. View
4. Exit
Select the item number:
```

---

set   **Manage shell options and the script's command-line parameters.**

```
set [options arg1 arg2 …]
```

With no arguments, set prints the values of all variables known to the current shell. Options can be enabled (-*option*) or disabled (+*option*). Options can also be set when the shell is invoked. (See the section "Invoking the Shell" on page 4.) Non-option arguments are assigned in order ($1, $2, etc.).

Options

- -a From now on, automatically mark variables for export after defining or changing them.

- -b Print job completion messages as soon as jobs terminate; don't wait until the next prompt.

- -B Enable brace expansion. On by default.

- -C Prevent overwriting via > redirection; use >| to overwrite files.

- -e Exit if a command yields a nonzero exit status. The ERR trap executes before the shell exits. The exact behavior is complicated; see "set -e Details" on page 118, later in this entry.

- -E Cause shell functions, command substitutions, and sub-shells to inherit the ERR trap.

- -f Ignore filename metacharacters (e.g., * ? [ ]).

-h   Locate commands as they are defined. On by default. See
      the entry for hash on page 98.

-H   Enable csh-style history substitution. On by default. (Bash
      5.0 will change this to be off by default.) See the section
      "C-Shell–Style History" on page 51.

-k   Assignment of environment variables (*var=value*) takes
      effect regardless of where they appear on the command
      line. Normally, assignments must precede the command
      name.

-m   Enable job control; background jobs execute in a separate
      process group. -m is usually set automatically; interactive
      shells enable it, scripts do not.

-n   Read commands but don't execute them; useful for check-
      ing syntax. Interactive shells ignore this option.

+o [*mode*]
      With *mode*, disable the given shell mode. Plain set +o
      prints the settings of all the current modes in a form that
      can be reread by the shell later.

-o [*mode*]
      List shell modes, or turn on mode *mode*. Many modes can
      be set by other options. Modes are:

allexport	Same as -a.
braceexpand	Same as -B.
emacs	Set command-line editor to emacs.
errexit	Same as -e.
errtrace	Same as -E.
functrace	Same as -T.
hashall	Same as -h.
histexpand	Same as -H.
history	Enable command history. On by default.

ignoreeof	Don't process *EOF* signals. To exit the shell, type `exit`.
keyword	Same as `-k`.
monitor	Same as `-m`.
noclobber	Same as `-C`.
noexec	Same as `-n`.
noglob	Same as `-f`.
nolog	Omit function definitions from the history file. Accepted but ignored by Bash.
notify	Same as `-b`.
nounset	Same as `-u`.
onecmd	Same as `-t`.
physical	Same as `-P`.
pipefail	Change pipeline exit status to be that of the rightmost command that failed, or zero if all exited successfully.
posix	Change to POSIX mode.
privileged	Same as `-p`.
verbose	Same as `-v`.
vi	Set command-line editor to `vi`.
xtrace	Same as `-x`.

+p   Reset effective UID to real UID.

-p   Start up as a privileged user. Don't read $ENV or $BASH_ENV, don't import functions from the environment, and ignore the values of the BASHOPTS, CDPATH, GLOBIGNORE, and SHELLOPTS variables.

-P   Always use physical paths for `cd` and `pwd`.

-t   Exit after executing one command.

-T   Cause shell functions, command substitutions, and sub-shells to inherit the DEBUG and RETURN traps.

- -u   In substitutions, treat unset variables as errors. However, references to $@ and $* are not errors when there are no positional parameters.

- -v   Show each shell command line when read.

- -x   Show commands and arguments when executed, preceded by the value of PS4. This provides step-by-step tracing of shell scripts.

- -   Turn off -v and -x, and turn off option processing. Included for compatibility with older versions of the Bourne shell.

- --   Used as the last option; -- turns off option processing so that arguments beginning with - are not misinterpreted as options. (For example, you can set $1 to -1.) If no arguments are given after --, unset the positional parameters.

Option Summary

Option	Same as
-a	-o allexport
-b	-o notify
-B	-o braceexpand
-C	-o noclobber
-e	-o errexit
-E	-o errtrace
-f	-o noglob
-h	-o hashall
-H	-o histexpand
-k	-o keyword
-m	-o monitor
-n	-o noexec

Option	Same as
-o allexport	-a
-o braceexpand	-B
-o emacs	
-o errexit	-e
-o errtrace	-E
-o functrace	-T
-o hashall	-h
-o history	
-o histexpand	-H
-o ignoreeof	
-o keyword	-k
-o monitor	-m
-o noclobber	-C
-o noexec	-n
-o noglob	-f
-o nolog	
-o notify	-b
-o nounset	-u
-o onecmd	-t
-o physical	-P
-o pipefail	
-o posix	
-o privileged	-p
-o verbose	-v
-o vi	
-o xtrace	-x

Option	Same as
-p	-o privileged
-P	-o physical
-t	-o onecmd
-T	-o functrace
-u	-o nounset
-v	-o verbose
-x	-o xtrace

set -e Details

When set -e is enabled, the shell exits if one of the following fails: a pipeline (which can be just a single command); a subshell command in parentheses; or any of the commands in a group enclosed in braces.

In POSIX mode, shells created to run command substitutions inherit the setting of set -e; otherwise such shells inherit the setting of set -e based on the setting of the inherit_errexit shell option.

Failure of a command (non-zero exit status) does not cause an exit in the following cases: Any command in a list following while or until; the pipeline following if or elif; any command in an && or || list except the last; any command in a pipeline but the last; or if the sense of the command's value is being inverted with !.

In general, shell programming experts consider set -e to be of little or no use in practical shell programming. It exists mostly for historical compatibility, and should not be used instead of careful programming to catch any and all errors that may occur.

Examples

```
set -- "$num" -20 -30    Set $1 to $num, $2 to -20, $3 to -30
set -vx                  Show each command twice; once when
                         read, and once when executed
set +x                   Stop command tracing
set -o noclobber         Prevent file overwriting
set +o noclobber         Allow file overwriting again
```

---

shift   Shift the command-line arguments left.

```
shift [n]
```

Shift positional arguments (e.g., $2 becomes $1). If *n* is given, shift to the left *n* places. Often used in while loops to iterate through the command-line arguments.

Example

```
shift $(($1 + $6))       Use expression result as shift count
```

---

shopt   Manage shell options.

```
shopt [-opqsu] [option]
```

Set or unset shell options. With no options or just -p, print the names and settings of the options. See the section "Shell Options" on page 60 for a description of the various options.

Options

-o   Each *option* must be one of the shell option names for set -o, instead of the options listed in the section "Shell Options" on page 60.

-p   Print the option settings as shopt commands that can be reread later.

-q Quiet mode. The exit status is zero if the given option is set, nonzero otherwise. With multiple options, all of them must be set for a zero exit status.

-s Set the given *options*. With no *options*, print only those that are set.

-u Unset the given *options*. With no *options*, print only those that are unset.

---

source   Read and execute a file within the current shell.

    source *file* [*arguments*]

Identical to the . (dot) command; see the entry for . on page 72 for more information.

---

suspend   Suspend the current shell.

    suspend [-f]

Suspend the current shell. Often used to stop an su command.

Option

-f Force the suspension, even if the shell is a login shell.

---

test   Evaluate conditions, for use in loops and conditionals.

    test *condition*
    [*condition*]
    [[*condition*]]

Evaluate a *condition* and, if its value is true, return a zero exit status; otherwise, return a nonzero exit status. An alternate form of the command uses [ ] rather than the word test. An

---

additional alternate form uses [[ ]], in which case word splitting and pathname expansion are not done (see the entry for [[ ]] on page 72). *condition* is constructed using the following expressions. Conditions are true if the description holds true.

File Conditions

-a *file*	*file* exists. (Deprecated; use - e instead.)
-b *file*	*file* exists and is a block special file.
-c *file*	*file* exists and is a character special file.
-d *file*	*file* exists and is a directory.
-e *file*	*file* exists. (Same as - a, for POSIX compatibility.)
-f *file*	*file* exists and is a regular file.
-g *file*	*file* exists, and its set-group-id bit is set.
-G *file*	*file* exists, and its group is the effective group ID.
-h *file*	*file* exists and is a symbolic link. (Same as - L.)
-k *file*	*file* exists, and its sticky bit is set.
-L *file*	*file* exists and is a symbolic link. (Same as - h.)
-N *file*	*file* exists and was modified after it was last read.
-O *file*	*file* exists, and its owner is the effective user ID.
-p *file*	*file* exists and is a named pipe (FIFO).
-r *file*	*file* exists and is readable.
-s *file*	*file* exists and has a size greater than zero.
-S *file*	*file* exists and is a socket.
-t [*n*]	The open file descriptor *n* is associated with a terminal device; default *n* is 1.
-u *file*	*file* exists, and its set-user-id bit is set.
-w *file*	*file* exists and is writable.
-x *file*	*file* exists and is executable.

f1 -ef *f2*   Files *f1* and *f2* are linked (refer to same file).

f1 -nt *f2*   File *f1* is newer than *f2*.

f1 -ot *f2*   File *f1* is older than *f2*.

String Conditions

string   *string* is not null.

-n *s1*   String *s1* has nonzero length.

-z *s1*   String *s1* has zero length.

s1 == *s2*   Strings *s1* and *s2* are identical. Inside [[ ]], *s2* can be a wildcard pattern. Quote *s2* to treat it literally. (See the section "Filename Metacharacters" on page 8. See also the nocasematch option in the section "Shell Options" on page 60.)

s1 = *s2*   Same as the == operator. Should be used with test and [ ] for compatibility with POSIX and other shells.

s1 != *s2*   Strings *s1* and *s2* are *not* identical. Inside [[ ]], *s2* can be a wildcard pattern. Quote *s2* to treat it literally.

s1 =~ *s2*   String *s1* matches extended regular expression *s2*. Only available inside [[ ]]. Quote *s2* to force string matching, instead of regular expression matching. Strings matched by parenthesized subexpressions are placed into elements of the BASH_REMATCH array. See the description of BASH_REMATCH in the section "Built-In Shell Variables" on page 32. See also the compat31, compat32, and compat40 options in the section "Shell Options" on page 60.

s1 < *s2*   String value of *s1* precedes that of *s2*. With test and [ ], you must quote the < and Bash uses the machine's sorting order (usually ASCII). With [[ ]], you don't have to quote the < and Bash uses the locale's sorting order.

s1 > *s2*   String value of *s1* follows that of *s2*. With test and [ ], you must quote the > and Bash uses the machine's sorting order (usually ASCII). With [[ ]], you don't have to quote the > and Bash uses the locale's sorting order.

Internal Shell Conditions

-o *opt*   Option *opt* for set -o is on.

-R *var*   Variable *var* has been assigned a value and is a nameref.

-v *var*   Variable *var* has been assigned a value. *var* may name an array element.

Integer Comparisons

n1 -eq *n2*   *n1* equals *n2*.

n1 -ge *n2*   *n1* is greater than or equal to *n2*.

n1 -gt *n2*   *n1* is greater than *n2*.

n1 -le *n2*   *n1* is less than or equal to *n2*.

n1 -lt *n2*   *n1* is less than *n2*.

n1 -ne *n2*   *n1* does not equal *n2*.

Combined Forms

(*condition*)

> True if *condition* is true (used for grouping). For test and [ ], the parentheses should be quoted by a \. The [[ ]] form doesn't require quoting the parentheses.

! *condition*

> True if *condition* is false.

condition1 -a *condition2*

> True if both conditions are true.

condition1 && *condition2*

> True if both conditions are true. Short-circuit form. (Use only within [[ ]].)

condition1 -o *condition2*

> True if either condition is true.

condition1 || *condition2*
> True if either condition is true. Short-circuit form. (Use only within [[ ]].)

Examples

The following examples show the first line of various statements that might use a test condition:

```
while test $# -gt 0          While there are arguments

if [ $count -lt 10 ]         If $count is less than 10
if [ -d .git ]               If the .git directory exists
if [ "$answer" != "y" ]      If the answer is not y
if [ ! -r "$1" -o ! -f "$1" ]   If the first argument is not
                                readable or a regular file
if ! [ -r "$1" ] || ! [ -f "$1" ]   Same as previous
```

---

time   Time a command.

```
time [-p] [command]
```

Execute *command* and print the total elapsed time, user time, and system time (in seconds). Same as the external command `time`, except that the built-in version can also time other built-in commands as well as all commands in a pipeline. The current locale's decimal point is used in the output.

With no *command*, print the elapsed user, system and real times for the shell and its children.

The value of the TIMEFORMAT variable controls the format of the output. See the *bash*(1) manual page for the details.

In POSIX mode, if the first argument begins with a minus sign, Bash treats `time` as a command, not as a keyword.

Option

-p Print the timing summary in the format specified by POSIX.

---

times   **Print accumulated CPU times.**

    times

Print accumulated user and system process times for the shell and the processes it has run.

---

trap   **Manage the disposition of signals within a shell script.**

    trap [[commands] signals]
    trap -l
    trap -p

Execute *commands* if any *signals* are received. The second form lists all signals and their numbers, like kill -l. The third form prints the current trap settings in a form suitable for rereading later. Signals ignored at shell startup are included, but cannot be changed.

Common signals include EXIT (0), HUP (1), INT (2), and TERM (15). Multiple commands must be quoted as a group and separated by semicolons internally. If *commands* is the null string (i.e., trap "" *signals*), cause the shell to ignore *signals*. If *commands* are omitted entirely, reset processing of specified signals to the default action. If *commands* is "-", reset *signals* to their initial defaults.

If both *commands* and *signals* are omitted, list the current trap assignments. See the Examples here and in the entry for exec on page 91.

Normally, trap prints signal names with a leading SIG prefix. In POSIX mode, it leaves off the prefix.

The shell does not block additional occurrences of signals for traps that are running, allowing recursive trap invocations. Use with care!

Tip

In general, *commands* should be quoted using single quotes, so that any variable or other substitutions are delayed until the signal is handled. Otherwise, with double quotes, the expansions are evaluated earlier, when the trap command itself executes.

Signals

For standard signals, the shell allows you to use either the signal number or the signal name (with or without the SIG prefix). In addition, the shell supports "pseudo-signals," signal names or numbers that aren't real operating system signals but which direct the shell to perform a specific action. These signals and when they execute are:

DEBUG   Execution of any command.

ERR   Nonzero exit status.

EXIT   Exit from shell (usually when shell script finishes). Also for shells started for process substitution.

RETURN   A return is executed, or a script run with . (dot) or source finishes.

0   Same as EXIT, for historical compatibility with the Bourne shell.

Examples

```
trap "" INT        Ignore interrupts (signal 2)
trap INT           Obey interrupts again
```

Remove a $tmp file when the shell program exits, or if the user logs out, presses CTRL-C, or does a kill:

```
trap "rm -f $tmp; exit" EXIT HUP INT TERM    POSIX style
trap "rm -f $tmp; exit" 0 1 2 15             Original shell
```

Print a "clean up" message when the shell program receives signals SIGHUP, SIGINT, or SIGTERM:

```
trap 'echo Interrupt!  Cleaning up...' HUP INT TERM
```

---

true   Exit with a true (success) return value.

```
true
```

Built-in command that exits with a true return value.

---

type   Print the type of a command.

```
type [-afpPt] commands
```

Show whether each command name is an external command, a built-in command, an alias, a shell keyword, or a defined shell function.

Options

- -a   Print all locations in $PATH that include *command*, including aliases and functions. Use -p together with -a to suppress aliases and functions.

- -f   Suppress function lookup, as with command.

- -p   If type -t would print file for a given *command*, print the full pathname for the corresponding executable file. Otherwise, print nothing.

- -P   Like -p, but force a search of $PATH, even if type -t would not print file.

-t   Print a word describing each *command*. The word is one
     of alias, builtin, file, function, or keyword, depending
     upon the type of each *command*.

Example

```
$ type mv read if
mv is /bin/mv
read is a shell builtin
if is a shell keyword
```

---

typeset   Declare shell variables and manage their attributes.

```
typeset [options] [variable[=value …]]
```

Identical to declare. See the entry for declare on page 85.

---

ulimit   Manage various process limits.

```
ulimit [options] [n]
```

Print the value of one or more resource limits, or, if *n* is specified, set a resource limit to *n*. Resource limits can be either hard
(-H) or soft (-S). By default, ulimit sets both limits or prints
the soft limit. The options determine which resource is acted
upon.

Options

-H   Hard limit. Anyone can lower a hard limit; only privileged
     users can raise it.

-S   Soft limit. Must be less than or equal to the hard limit.

-a   Print all limits.

-b   Maximum size of a socket buffer.

- -c   Maximum size of core files. Default units are 1K-byte blocks. In POSIX mode, units are 512-byte blocks.

- -d   Maximum kilobytes of data segment or heap.

- -e   Maximum scheduling priority (nice value).

- -f   Maximum size of files (the default option). Default units are 1K-byte blocks. In POSIX mode, units are 512-byte blocks.

- -i   Maximum number of pending signals.

- -k   Maximum number of kqueues. (Not effective on all systems.)

- -l   Maximum size of address space that can be locked in memory.

- -m   Maximum kilobytes of physical memory. (Not effective on all systems.)

- -n   Maximum number of file descriptors.

- -p   Size of pipe buffers. (Not effective on all systems.)

- -P   Maximum number of pseudoterminals. (Not effective on all systems.)

- -q   Maximum number of bytes in POSIX message queues.

- -r   Maximum real-time scheduling priority.

- -s   Maximum kilobytes of stack segment.

- -t   Maximum CPU seconds.

- -T   Maximum number of threads.

- -u   Maximum number of processes a single user can have.

- -v   Maximum kilobytes of virtual memory. (Not effective on all systems.)

- -x   Maximum number of file locks.

umask

```
umask [nnn]
umask [-pS] [mask]
```

Display the file creation mask or set the file creation mask to octal value *nnn*. The file creation mask determines which permission bits are turned off (e.g., umask 002 produces rw-rw-r--). For the second form, a symbolic mask represents permissions to keep.

Options

-p   Output is in a form that can be reread later by the shell.

-S   Print the current mask using symbolic notation.

unalias

```
unalias names
unalias -a
```

Remove *names* from the alias list. See also the entry for alias on page 74.

Option

-a   Remove all aliases.

unset

```
unset [options] names
```

Erase definitions of functions or variables listed in *names*. A *name* subscripted with an index (unset foo[2]) unsets the corresponding array element. An index of 0 unsets the related scalar variable.

Options

-f   Unset functions *names*.

-n   Unset nameref variables *names*. See the section "Indirect Variables (namerefs)" on page 31.

-v   Unset variables *names* (default).

---

until   **Syntax for a loop that runs until a condition becomes true.**

```
until condition
do
      commands
done
```

Until *condition* is met, do *commands*. *condition* is often specified with the test command. See the Examples under the entries for case on page 77, and test on page 120.

---

wait   **Wait for a process or job to complete.**

```
wait [-n] [ID]
```

With no option or arguments, pause in execution until all background jobs complete and then return an exit status of zero. With *ID*, pause until the specified background process *ID* or job *ID* completes and then return its exit status. Note that the shell variable $! contains the process ID of the most recent background process.

With no arguments, wait's behavior depends upon the setting of POSIX mode. Normally, wait waits for all backgrounded processes to finish, and then runs the SIGCHLD trap as many times as there were exited processes. In POSIX mode, an exiting child interrupts wait, causing it to exit with 128 + SIGCHLD. Bash attempts to run the SIGCHLD trap handler once for each exiting child, but it does not guarantee that it will do so.

Option

-n Wait for any job to terminate and return its exit status.

Example

wait $!   *Wait for most recent background process to finish*

---

while   Syntax for a loop that runs while a condition remains true.

```
while condition
do
    commands
done
```

While *condition* is met, do *commands*. *condition* is often specified with the test command. See the Examples under the entries for case on page 77, and test on page 120.

---

filename   Run an external command.

filename [arguments]

Read and execute commands from executable file *filename*, or execute a binary object file. If *filename* does not contain any slash characters, the shell searches for the file to execute in the directories listed in $PATH.

Resources

This section briefly describes other sources of information about or related to Bash.

Online Resources

http://ftp.gnu.org/gnu/bash
> The top-level directory for Bash source code releases. Source code is usually made available as *.tar.gz* files, such as *bash-4.4.tar.gz*.

ftp://ftp.gnu.org/pub/gnu/bash/bash-4.4-patches
> Patches for Bash 4.4 are in this directory.

http://www.gnu.org/software/bash/bash.html
http://tiswww.tis.cwru.edu/~chet/bash/bashtop.html
> The two "home pages" for the Bash shell.

http://bashdb.sourceforge.net
> The Bash debugger.

http://bash-completion.alioth.debian.org/
> Ian Macdonald's collected set of completion specifications.

http://www.gnu.org/software/bash/manual/html_node/Bash-POSIX-Mode.html
> Full documentation on the effects of POSIX mode. Many of the differences are subtle and don't affect most day-to-day uses of the shell.

http://www.opengroup.org/onlinepubs/9699919799
> The online version of the POSIX standard.

http://tobold.org/article/rc
> The rc shell for Unix systems.

Books

Newham, Cameron. *Learning the bash Shell*, Third Edition. Sebastopol: O'Reilly Media, 2005.

Robbins, Arnold, and Nelson H.F. Beebe. *Classic Shell Scripting*. Sebastopol: O'Reilly Media, 2005.

Acknowledgments

Thanks to Chet Ramey, the Bash maintainer, for providing access to early releases of Bash 4.4, for answering questions, and for yet again reviewing this reference. Thanks to Robert P.J. Day for again reviewing this work. Thanks to Eli Zaretskii for comments on the previous edition and for reviewing this edition. Thanks to Andy Oram at O'Reilly Media for his support of this update.

Acknowledgments from the First Edition

Thanks to Chet Ramey, the Bash maintainer, for providing access to early releases of Bash 4.1, and for once again reviewing this reference. Thanks to Robert P.J. Day for reviewing this edition. Thanks again to Mike Loukides at O'Reilly Media for his continued support of this project.

Index

Symbols

! (exclamation mark)
    != inequality operator, 48
    event designators, 52
    filename metacharacter, 9
    logical negation operator, 48
" (quotation marks, double)
    " " quoting, 14
    $" " quoting, 15
    escape sequence, 13
(hash mark), comments, 14, 70
#!shell command, 71
$ (dollar sign)
    $( ) command substitution, 16
    $(( )) arithmetic substitution, 16
    ${ } variable substitution, 27
    last argument, 52
    shell variables, 32
    variable substitution, 14
% (percent)
    argument matched by, 52
    job control, 59
    modulus operator, 48
& (ampersand)
    && logical AND operator, 48, 73
    background execution, 14
    bitwise AND operator, 48
' (quotation marks, single)
    $' ' quoting, 13
    ' ' quoting, 14
    escape sequence, 13
() (parentheses), command grouping, 14
* (asterisk)
    ** exponentiation operator, 48
    ** filename metacharacters, 9
    all arguments, 53
    filename metacharacter, 8
    multiplication operator, 48
+ (plus sign)
    ++ auto-increment operator, 48
    += operator, 26
    addition operator, 48
    filename metacharacter, 9
    unary operator, 48
, (comma), sequential expression evaluation operator, 48
- (hyphen)
    -- auto-decrement operator, 48
    filename metacharacter, 8

subtraction operator, 48
unary operator, 48
. (dot), read and execute files, 72
.bashrc file, 8
.bash_history file, 40
.bash_login file, 8
.bash_logout file, 8, 92, 105
.bash_profile file, 8
    shell variables, 38
.inputrc file, 41, 75, 76
.profile file, 4, 8, 69
    shell variables, 38
/ (slash), division operator, 48
/etc/bash_completion file, 57
/etc/passwd file, 8, 41
/etc/profile file, 4, 6, 8, 69
: (colon)
    :0 command name, 52
    :n argument number, 52
    :... history and truncation
        modifiers, 53
    do-nothing command, 71
; (semicolon)
    ;& case terminator, 78
    ;;& case terminator, 78
    command separator, 14
< (left angle bracket)
    << bitwise shift left operator,
        48
    <<= assignment operator, 48
    <= less than or equal to oper-
        ator, 48
    less than operator, 48, 73
<, > (angle brackets), redirection
    symbols, 14
= (equals sign)
    == equality operator, 48
    assignment operator, 26
> (right angle bracket)
    >= greater than or equal to
        operator, 48
    >> bitwise shift right opera-
        tor, 48

>>= assignment operator, 48
greater than operator, 48, 73
? (question mark)
    ?: inline conditional evalua-
        tion operator, 48
    escape sequence, 13
    filename metacharacter, 8
@ (at sign), filename metachar-
    acter, 9
[ ] (brackets)
    filename metacharacters, 8
    [[ ]] test command, 72
\ (backslash)
    escape sequence, 13
    prompt strings, 46
    quoting, 14, 15
\! prompt string, 47
\" escape sequence, 13
\# prompt string, 47
\$ prompt string, 47
\& in completion patterns, 56
\0 escape sequence, 13
\? escape sequence, 13
\@ prompt string, 47
\a escape sequence, 13
\a prompt string, 46
\A prompt string, 46
\b escape sequence, 13
\c escape sequence, 13
\cX escape sequence, 13
\d prompt string, 46
\D prompt string, 46
\e escape sequence, 13
\E escape sequence, 13
\e prompt string, 46
\f escape sequence, 13
\h prompt string, 46
\H prompt string, 46
\J prompt string, 46
\l prompt string, 46
\n escape sequence, 13
\n prompt string, 46
\nnn escape sequence, 13

\nnn prompt string, 47
\r escape sequence, 13
\r prompt string, 46
\s prompt string, 46
\t escape sequence, 13
\t prompt string, 46
\T prompt string, 46
\u escape sequence, 13
\U escape sequence, 13
\u prompt string, 46
\v escape sequence, 13
\v prompt string, 46
\V prompt string, 46
\w prompt string, 43, 46
\W prompt string, 43, 46
\x escape sequence, 13
\[prompt string, 47
\\ escape sequence, 13
\\ prompt string, 47
\] prompt string, 47
\' escape sequence, 13
^ (caret)
    bitwise exclusive OR operator, 48
    first argument, 52
` (backquote), command substitution, 14
| (pipe character)
    bitwise OR operator, 48
    pipe command, 70
    quoting, 14
    || logical OR operator, 48, 73
~ (tilde), filename metacharacter, 8

A

addition operator, 48
alert escape sequence, 13
alias command, 74
aliases, removing, 130
alnum class, 9
alpha class, 9

alphabetic characters, filename metacharacter, 9
alphanumeric characters, filename metacharacter, 9
ampersand (&)
    && logical AND operator, 48, 73
    background execution, 14
    bitwise AND operator, 48
AND operators, 48
angle brackets (<, >), redirection symbols, 14
arguments
    Bash shell, 6
    job control commands, 59
    printing, 88, 107
    shifting command-line arguments left, 119
arithmetic operations, let command, 47, 104
arithmetic operators, 47
arrays
    associative arrays, 45
    indexed arrays, 44
    reading files into, 105, 111
ASCII characters, filename metacharacter, 9
ascii class, 9
associative arrays, 45
asterisk (*)
    ** exponentiation operator, 48
    ** filename metacharacters, 9
    all arguments, 53
    filename metacharacter, 8
    multiplication operator, 48
at sign (@), filename metacharacter, 9
attributes, shell variables, 85
auto-decrement operator, 48
autocd shell option, 60
auto_resume shell variable, 44

B

background jobs
    putting current job into background, 74
    running or suspending, 95
backquote (`), command substitution, 14
backslash (\)
    escape sequence, 13
    prompt strings, 46
    quoting, 14, 15
Bash (Bourne-Again shell)
    arithmetic expressions, 47
    built-in commands, 70-132
    command execution, 66
    command exit status, 6-7
    command history, 49-54
    coprocesses, 68
    features, 3
    functions, 23
    history of, 3
    invoking Bash shell, 4
    job control, 59
    options, 60-66
    programmable completion, 54-58
    restricted shells, 69
    syntax, 7-23
    variables, 25-47
BASH shell variable, 33
BASHOPTS shell variable, 33
BASHPID shell variable, 33
.bashrc file, 8
BASH_ALIASES shell variable, 33
BASH_ARGC shell variable, 33
BASH_ARGV shell variable, 34
BASH_CMDS shell variable, 34
BASH_COMMAND shell variable, 34
BASH_COMPAT shell variable, 38
BASH_ENV shell variable, 38

BASH_EXECUTION_STRING shell variable, 34
.bash_history file, 40
BASH_LINENO shell variable, 34
BASH_LOADABLES_PATH shell variable, 39
.bash_login file, 8
.bash_logout file, 8, 92, 105
.bash_profile file, 8
    shell variables, 38
BASH_REMATCH shell variable, 34
BASH_SOURCE shell variable, 34
BASH_SUBSHELL shell variable, 35
BASH_VERSINFO shell variable, 35
BASH_VERSION shell variable, 35
BASH_XTRACEFD shell variable, 39
Berkeley C shell, history of, 2
bg command, 59, 74
bind command, 75
bitwise AND operator, 48
bitwise exclusive OR operator, 48
bitwise OR operator, 48
bitwise shift left operator, 48
bitwise shift right operator, 48
blank class, 9
Bourne shell, history of, 2
brace expansion, syntax, 11
brackets [ ]
    filename metacharacters, 8
    [[ ]] test command, 72
break command, 76
built-in shell variables, 32
builtin command, 76

C

caller command, 77
caret (^)

bitwise exclusive OR operator, 48
  first argument, 52
carriage return escape sequence, 13
case command, 77
case statements, esac command, 90
cd command, 78
cdable_vars shell option, 61
CDPATH shell variable, 39
cdspell shell option, 61
checkhash shell option, 61
checkjobs shell option, 61
checkwinsize shell option, 61
CHILD_MAX shell variable, 39
cmdhist shell option, 61
cntrl class, 9
colon (:)
  :0 command name, 52
  :n argument number, 52
  :… history and truncation modifiers, 53
  do-nothing command, 71
COLUMNS shell variable, 39
comma (,), sequential expression evaluation operator, 48
command command, 79
command exit status, 6-7
command forms, syntax, 16
command history, 49-54
  C-shell–style history, 51
  fc command, 51
  line-edit mode, 50
command line
  editor, 50
  history, 93, 100
  manipulation in Bash, 50
  options, 97
  printing arguments, 107
  script parameters, 113
commands, 70-132
  #!shell command, 71

: do-nothing command, 71
bg command, 59, 74
bind command, 75
break command, 76
builtin command, 76
caller command, 77
case command, 77
cd command, 78
command command, 79
compgen command, 54, 80
complete command, 54, 80
compopt command, 57, 84
continue command, 85
declare command, 85
dirs command, 87
disown command, 87
do command, 88
done command, 88
echo command, 88
enable command, 89
enabling and disabling, 89
esac command, 90
eval command, 90
exec command, 91
executing, 66
exit command, 92
export command, 92
external commands, 132
false command, 93
fc command, 51, 93
fg command, 59, 95
fi command, 95
filename command, 132
for command, 95
function command, 97
getopts command, 97
hash command, 98
help command, 99
history command, 49, 100
if command, 101
job control, 59
jobs command, 59, 102
kill command, 60, 103

let command, 104
local command, 105
logout command, 105
man command, 58
mapfile command, 105
name ( ) command, 74
popd command, 106
printf command, 107
pushd command, 108
pwd command, 108
read command, 109, 111
readonly command, 111
return command, 24, 112
select command, 112
set command, 113-118
shift command, 119
shopt command, 60, 119
source command, 120
stty command, 60
suspend command, 60, 120
test command, 120-124
time command, 124
times command, 125
trap command, 125
true command, 127
type command, 127
typeset command, 128
ulimit command, 128
umask command, 130
unalias command, 130
unset command, 130
until command, 131
wait command, 60, 131
while command, 132
[[ ]] test command, 72
comments, # (hash mark), 14, 70
comparisons, integers, 123
compat31 shell option, 61
compat32 shell option, 61
compat40 shell option, 62
compat41 shell option, 62
compat42 shell option, 62
compat43 shell option, 62

compgen command, 54, 80
complete command, 54, 80
complete_fullquote shell option,
    62
completion facilities, 51, 54, 80
completion, programmable,
    54-58
compopt command, 57, 84
COMPREPLY shell variable, 39
compspecs, programmable com-
    pletion, 55
COMP_CWORD shell variable,
    35
COMP_KEY shell variable, 35
COMP_LINE shell variable, 35
COMP_POINT shell variable, 35
COMP_TYPE shell variable, 35
COMP_WORDBREAKS shell
    variable, 35
COMP_WORDS shell variable,
    36
conditions, evaluating, 120
continue command, 85
control characters, filename met-
    acharacter, 9
COPROC shell variable, 36
coprocesses, 68
CPU times, 125
csh (Berkeley C shell), history, 2
CTRL-Z job control command,
    59, 60

D
DEBUG trap, 24
decimal digits, filename meta-
    character, 9
declare command, 85
declaring
    variables, 85, 128
digit class, 9
directories
    changing, 78

popping directories off directory stack, 106

pushing directories onto directory stack, 108

search path for changing, 39

working directories, 108

directory stack

popping directories off directory stack, 106

printing or managing, 87

pushing directories onto directory stack, 108

direxpand shell option, 62

dirs command, 87

dirspell shell option, 62

DIRSTACK shell variable, 36

disabling commands, 89

disown command, 87

division operator, 48

do command, 88

do-nothing command (:), 71

dollar sign ($)

$( ) command substitution, 16

$(( )) arithmetic substitution, 16

${ } variable substitution, 27

last argument, 52

shell variables, 32

variable substitution, 14

done command, 88

dot (.), read and execute files, 72

dotglob shell option, 62

dynamic scoping, 25

E

echo command, 88

editing, keyboard shortcuts for, 50

Emacs editor, Bash command-line editing mode, 50

EMACS shell variable, 39

enable command, 89

$ENV file (read by Bash shell at startup), 8

ENV shell variable, 39

equals sign (=)

== equality operator, 48

assignment operator, 26

ERR trap, 25

esac command, 90

escape sequences, quoted text ($' '), 15

EUID shell variable, 36

eval command, 90

evaluating conditions, 120

event designators, 52

exclamation mark (!)

!= inequality operator, 48

event designators, 52

filename metacharacter, 9

logical negation operator, 48

exec command, 91

execfail shell option, 63

EXECIGNORE shell variable, 39

executing

commands, 66

files, 72, 120

input lines, 90

exit command, 92

exit status, 6

$? variable, 6

nonzero, 6

of shell functions, 112

success and failure, 6

true and false, 6

zero, 6

EXIT trap, 25

exiting

kill command, 103

shell, 105

shell scripts, 92

with a false return value, 93

with a true return value, 127

expand_aliases shell option, 63

exponentiation operator, 48

export command, 92
expressions, arithmetic, 47
extdebug shell option, 63
extglob shell option, 39, 40, 63
extquote shell option, 63

F

failglob shell option, 64
false command, 93
fc command, 51, 93
FCEDIT shell variable, 40, 94
fg command, 59, 95
fi command, 95
FIGNORE shell variable, 40
filename command, 132
filenames
    metacharacters, 8
    redirection forms, 22
files
    creation mask, 130
    evaluating conditions, 121
    reading and executing, 72,
        120
    reading into arrays, 105, 111
for command, 95
force_fignore shell option, 64
formfeed escape sequence, 13
forms, combined forms, 123
    (see also redirection forms)
FUNCNAME shell variable, 36
FUNCNEST shell variable, 36
function command, 97
functions
    about, 23
    defining, 73
    exit status of, 112
    getpwnam() C function, 8
    getpwuid() C function, 8
    parsing, 10
    removing, 130
    traps, 24
    variable scoping, 25

G

getconf command, 96
getopts command, 97
getpwnam() C function, 8
getpwuid() C function, 8
globasciiranges shell option, 64
GLOBIGNORE shell variable, 40
globstar shell option, 64
gnu_errfmt shell option, 64
graph class, 9
greater than operator, 48
greater than or equal to operator,
    48
GROUPS shell variable, 36

H

hash command, 98
hash mark (#), comments, 14, 70
help command, 99
here document, 18
here string, 18
hexadecimal escape sequence, 13
histappend shell option, 64
histchars shell variable, 44
HISTCMD shell variable, 36
HISTCONTROL shell variable,
    40
HISTFILE shell variable, 40
HISTFILESIZE shell variable, 40
HISTIGNORE shell variable, 40
history
    command history, 49-54, 93,
        100
    history modifiers, 53
history command, 49, 100
histreedit shell option, 64
HISTSIZE shell variable, 40
HISTTIMEFORMAT shell vari-
    able, 41
histverify shell option, 64
HOME shell variable, 41
hostcomplete shell option, 64
HOSTFILE shell variable, 41

HOSTNAME shell variable, 36
HOSTTYPE shell variable, 36
huponexit shell option, 65
hyphen (-)
    -- auto-decrement operator,
      48
    option terminator, 6
    subtraction operator, 48
    unary operator, 48

I

if statement, 95, 101
IFS shell variable, 41
IGNOREEOF shell variable, 41
indexed arrays, 44
indirect variables, 31
inequality operator, 48
inherit_errexit shell option, 65,
    118
inline conditional evaluation
    operator, 48
input lines, rescan or execute, 90
.inputrc file, 41, 75, 76
INPUTRC shell variable, 41
integers, comparisons, 123
interactive_comments shell
    option, 65
interpreters, invoking, 71
invoking
    Bash shell, 4
    interpreters, 71

J

job control, 59
jobID argument, 59
jobs
    background jobs, 74, 95
    list running or stopped jobs,
      102
    stop managing, 87
    stopping, 103
    wait command, 131

jobs command, 59, 102

K

keyboard shortcuts for editing, 50
kill command, 60, 103

L

LANG shell variable, 41
lastpipe shell option, 65
LC_ALL shell variable, 41
LC_COLLATE shell variable, 41
LC_CTYPE shell variable, 41
LC_MESSAGES shell variable, 41
LC_NUMERIC shell variable, 41
LC_TIME shell variable, 41
left angle bracket (<)
    << bitwise shift left operator,
      48
    <<= assignment operator, 48
    <= less than or equal to oper-
      ator, 48
    less than operator, 48, 73
less than operator, 48
less than or equal to operator, 48
let command, 47, 104
line-edit mode (command his-
    tory), 50
LINENO shell variable, 36
LINES shell variable, 41
/bin/sh, link to Bash, 4
lithist shell option, 65
local command (local variables),
    105
logical AND operator, 48, 73
logical negation operator, 48
logical OR operator, 48
login_shell shell option, 65
logout command, 105
loops
    breaking out, 76
    continuing, 85
    do command, 88

done command, 88
for command, 95
select command, 112
until command, 131
while command, 132
lower class, 10
lowercase characters, filename
    metacharacter, 10

M

MACHTYPE shell variable, 36
MAIL shell variable, 42
MAILCHECK shell variable, 42
MAILPATH shell variable, 42
mailwarn shell option, 65
man command, 58
mapfile command, 105
MAPFILE shell variable, 37
masks, file creation mask, 130
metacharacters, Bash shell file-
    names, 8
modulus operator, 48
multiple redirection, 19
multiplication operator, 48

N

nameref variables, 31
newline
    escape sequence, 13
    word separator, 14
nocaseglob shell option, 65
nocasematch shell option, 27, 40,
    56, 65, 78
nonspace characters, filename
    metacharacter, 9
nonzero exit status, 6
no_empty_cmd_completion shell
    option, 65
nullglob shell option, 66

O

octal value escape sequence, 13

OLDPWD shell variable, 37
OpenVMS, 1
operators
    += operator, 26
    arithmetic operators, 47
OPTARG shell variable, 37
OPTERR shell variable, 42
OPTIND shell variable, 37
OR operators, 48
OSTYPE shell variable, 37

P

parentheses (), command group-
    ing, 14
parsing
    of functions, 10
    of scripts, 10
PATH shell variable, 42
percent (%)
    argument matched by, 52
    job control, 59
    modulus operator, 48
pipe character (|)
    bitwise OR operator, 48
    pipe command, 70
    || logical OR operator, 48, 73
PIPESTATUS shell variable, 37
plus sign (+)
    ++ auto-increment operator,
        48
    += operator, 26
    addition operator, 48
    filename metacharacter, 9
    unary operator, 48
popd command, 106
POSIX differences
    aliases for keywords, 66
    command execution order, 67
    command line assignments,
        80
    echo command, 89
    extglob shell option, 63
    fc command, 40, 94

function naming, 25
hash command, 98
history expansion, 51
inherit_errexit shell option, 65
kill command, 104
process substitution, 21
prompting, 47
read command, 109
searching $PATH, 72
set -e inheritance, 118
startup file, 8
tilde in $PATH, 67
time command, 124
trap command, 125
ulimit command, 129
variable substitution and nested quotes, 27
wait command, 131
POSIXLY_CORRECT shell variable, 42
postfix texts (brace expansion), 11
PPID shell variable, 37
prefix texts (brace expansion), 11
printable characters, filename metacharacter, 10
printf command, 107
printing
    command usage information, 99
    command-line history, 100
    working directories, 108
process substitution, 20
.profile file, 4, 8, 69
    shell variables, 38
progcomp shell option, 66
programmable completion, 54-58
prompt strings, 46
promptvars shell option, 66
PROMPT_COMMAND shell variable, 42
PROMPT_DIRTRIM shell variable, 43

PS0-PS4 shell variables, 43
punctuation characters, filename metacharacter, 10
pushd command, 108
pwd command, 108
PWD shell variable, 37

Q
question mark (?)
    ?: inline conditional evaluation operator, 48
    escape sequence, 13
    filename metacharacter, 8
quotation marks, double (")
    " " quoting, 14
    $" " quoting, 15
    escape sequence, 13
quotation marks, single (')
    $' ' quoting, 13
    ' ' quoting, 14
    escape sequence, 13
quoting, syntax, 14

R
RANDOM shell variable, 37
read command, 109
readarray command, 111
reading, files, 72, 105, 111, 120
readline library, bindings, 75
READLINE_LINE shell variable, 37
READLINE_POINT shell variable, 37
readonly command, 111
redirection forms, 17-23
    multiple redirection, 19
    process substitution, 20
    redirection using file descriptors, 19
    simple redirection, 17
    special filenames, 22
    standard error, 17

standard input, 17
standard output, 17
referencing arrays, 45
removing
   aliases, 130
   functions, 130
   variables, 130
REPLY shell variable, 37, 109
rescanning input lines, 90
resources, 133
restricted shells, 69
restricted_shell shell option, 66
return command, 24, 112
RETURN trap, 25
return values
   exiting with a false return
      value, 93
   exiting with a true return
      value, 127
right angle bracket (>)
   >= greater than or equal to
      operator, 48
   >> bitwise shift right opera-
      tor, 48
   >>= assignment operator, 48
   greater than operator, 48, 73

S

scoping
   dynamic, 25
   variables, 25
scripts
   command-line parameters,
      113
   exiting, 92
   parsing, 10
   replacing, 91
   signals, 125
select command, 112
semicolon (;)
   ;& case terminator, 78
   ;;& case terminator, 78
   command separator, 14

set command, 113-118
sh, invoking Bash as, 4
SHELL shell variable, 43
SHELLOPTS shell variable, 37
shells, 3
   (see also Bash)
   Bourne shell, 2
   declaring variables, 85
   evaluating conditions, 123
   invoking Bash shell, 4
   managing options, 119
   options, 60-66, 113
   restricted shells, 69
   suspending, 120
shift command, 119
shift_verbose shell option, 66
SHLVL shell variable, 38
shopt command, 60, 119
signal-based traps, 24
signals, shell scripts, 125
slash (/), division operator, 48
source command, 120
sourcepath shell option, 66, 72
space character
   filename metacharacter, 9
   word separator, 14
stacks, directory stack, 87, 106,
   108
standard error, redirection forms,
   17
standard input, redirection forms,
   17
standard output, redirection
   forms, 17
status, exit, 6
stopping jobs, 103
   (see also exiting)
strings
   completions, 80
   default variable value, 26
   evaluating conditions, 122
   prompt strings, 46
stty command, 60

substitution
   arithmetic, 16, 47
   command, 16
   PS0-PS4 shell variables, 47
   variables, 27
   word substitution, 52
subtraction operator, 48
suspend command, 60, 120
syntax, 7-23
   Bash arguments, 6
   brace expansion, 11
   command forms, 16
   filename metacharacters, 8
   quoting, 14
   redirection forms, 17-23
   special files, 8
System V, Bourne shell, 2

T

tab character, filename metacharacter, 9
tab escape sequence, 13
tab word separator, 14
TERM shell variable, 43
test command, 72, 120-124
tilde (~), filename metacharacter, 8
time command, 124
TIMEFORMAT shell variable, 43
times command, 125
tip
   #! line length limit, 71
   /etc/bash_completion file, 57
   avoid restricted shells, 69
   changing script parsing, 10
   clearing the hash table, 99
   exit within functions, 25
   interactive editing vs. fc command, 51
   keeping the history file up-to-date, 101
   prefer functions to aliases, 74

   quoting with the trap command, 126
   restricting completion to help topics, 84
TMOUT shell variable, 43
TMPDIR shell variable, 43
trap command, 125
traps, list of, 24
true command, 127
truncation modifiers, 53
type command, 127
typeset command, 128

U

UID shell variable, 38
ulimit command, 128
umask command, 130
unalias command, 130
unary operators, 48
unset command, 130
until command, 131
upper class, 10
uppercase characters, filename metacharacter, 10

V

variable scoping, 25
variables, 25-47
   arrays, 44
   assignment, 26
   built-in shell variables, 32
   declaring, 85, 128
   exporting or printing info about, 92
   local variables, 105
   other shell variables, 38
   prompt strings, 46
   read-only, 111
   reading, 109
   removing, 130
   substitution, 27
vertical tab escape sequence, 13

vi editor, Bash command-line editing mode, 50
VMS, 1

W

wait command, 60, 131
while command, 132
whitespace characters, filename metacharacter, 10

word substitution, 52
working directories, printing, 108

X

xpg_echo shell option, 66

Z

zero exit status, 6

About the Author

Arnold Robbins is a professional programmer and technical author who has worked with Unix systems since 1980 and has been using Awk since 1987. As a member of the POSIX 1003.2 balloting group, he helped shape the POSIX standard for Awk. Arnold is the maintainer of GNU Awk (`gawk`) and its documentation. He is the author of the fourth edition of *Effective awk Programming* and the coauthor of *Classic Shell Scripting* (both published by O'Reilly).

The information you need, when and where you need it.

With Safari Books Online, you can:

Access the contents of thousands of technology and business books

- Quickly search over 7000 books and certification guides
- Download whole books or chapters in PDF format, at no extra cost, to print or read on the go
- Copy and paste code
- Save up to 35% on O'Reilly print books
- **New!** Access mobile-friendly books directly from cell phones and mobile devices

Stay up-to-date on emerging topics before the books are published

- Get on-demand access to evolving manuscripts.
- Interact directly with authors of upcoming books

Explore thousands of hours of video on technology and design topics

- Learn from expert video tutorials
- Watch and replay recorded conference sessions

safaribooksonline.com

Get even more for your money.

Join the O'Reilly Community, and register the O'Reilly books you own. It's free, and you'll get:

- $4.99 ebook upgrade offer
- 40% upgrade offer on O'Reilly print books
- Membership discounts on books and events
- Free lifetime updates to ebooks and videos
- Multiple ebook formats, DRM FREE
- Participation in the O'Reilly community
- Newsletters
- Account management
- 100% Satisfaction Guarantee

Signing up is easy:

1. Go to: oreilly.com/go/register
2. Create an O'Reilly login.
3. Provide your address.
4. Register your books.

Note: English-language books only

To order books online:
oreilly.com/store

For questions about products or an order:
orders@oreilly.com

To sign up to get topic-specific email announcements and/or news about upcoming books, conferences, special offers, and new technologies:
elists@oreilly.com

For technical questions about book content:
booktech@oreilly.com

To submit new book proposals to our editors:
proposals@oreilly.com

O'Reilly books are available in multiple DRM-free ebook formats. For more information:
oreilly.com/ebooks